Glenn Gould
(1932–1982)

Vladimir Konieczny

Vladimir Konieczny was born in a refugee camp in Germany in 1946. He immigrated to Canada with his parents in 1950 and shortly after began accordion and piano lessons. During the 1960s and early 1970s, he competed in many music festivals and also played in clubs in Toronto before attending Wilfrid Laurier University, where he studied philosophy.

A former teacher of English and music for the Vancouver School Board, he now works as a freelance writer and as an instructor in Simon Fraser University's Writing and Publishing Program. Vladimir plays saxophone in a jazz combo and bassoon in two chamber ensembles and the Salt Spring Island Concert Band. He first heard Glenn Gould on the CBC during his teens, and has remained a lifelong fan of the pianist's music. In 2004, Vladimir published *Struggling for Perfection: The Story of Glenn Gould*, which was nominated for the Red Cedar Book Award.

In the Same Collection

Ven Begamudré, *Isaac Brock: Larger Than Life*
Lynne Bowen, *Robert Dunsmuir: Laird of the Mines*
Kate Braid, *Emily Carr: Rebel Artist*
Kathryn Bridge, *Phyllis Munday: Mountaineer*
William Chalmers, *George Mercer Dawson: Geologist, Scientist, Explorer*
Anne Cimon, *Susanna Moodie: Pioneer Author*
Deborah Cowley, *Lucille Teasdale: Doctor of Courage*
Gary Evans, *John Grierson: Trailblazer of Documentary Film*
Judith Fitzgerald, *Marshall McLuhan: Wise Guy*
lian goodall, *William Lyon Mackenzie King: Dreams and Shadows*
Stephen Eaton Hume, *Frederick Banting: Hero, Healer, Artist*
Naïm Kattan, *A.M. Klein: Poet and Prophet*
Betty Keller, *Pauline Johnson: First Aboriginal Voice of Canada*
Heather Kirk, *Mazo de la Roche: Rich and Famous Writer*
Michelle Labrèche-Larouche, *Emma Albani: International Star*
Wayne Larsen, *A.Y. Jackson: A Love for the Land*
Wayne Larsen, *James Wilson Morrice: Painter of Light and Shadow*
Francine Legaré, *Samuel de Champlain: Father of New France*
Margaret Macpherson, *Nellie McClung: Voice for the Voiceless*
Dave Margoshes, *Tommy Douglas: Building the New Society*
Marguerite Paulin, *René Lévesque: Charismatic Leader*
Marguerite Paulin, *Maurice Duplessis: Powerbroker, Politician*
Raymond Plante, *Jacques Plante: Behind the Mask*
T.F. Rigelhof, *George Grant: Redefining Canada*
Tom Shardlow, *David Thompson: A Trail by Stars*
Arthur Slade, *John Diefenbaker: An Appointment with Destiny*
Roderick Stewart, *Wilfrid Laurier: A Pledge for Canada*
Sharon Stewart, *Louis Riel: Firebrand*
André Vanasse, *Gabrielle Roy: A Passion for Writing*
John Wilson, *John Franklin: Traveller on Undiscovered Seas*
John Wilson, *Norman Bethune: A Life of Passionate Conviction*
Rachel Wyatt, *Agnes Macphail: Champion of the Underdog*

Copyright © Vladimir Konieczny, 2009

All rights reserved. No part of this publication may be reproduced, stored in a retrieval system, or transmitted in any form or by any means, electronic, mechanical, photocopying, recording, or otherwise (except for brief passages for purposes of review) without the prior permission of Dundurn Press. Permission to photocopy should be requested from Access Copyright.

Editor and Chronology: Rhonda Bailey
Copy-Editor: Allison Hirst
Index: Darcy Dunton
Design: Jennifer Scott
Printer: Webcom

Cover photo derived from Library and Archives Canada/e008293728. Courtesy of the Glenn Gould Estate.

Library and Archives Canada Cataloguing in Publication

Konieczny, Vladimir, 1946-
    Glenn Gould : a musical force / Vladimir Konieczny.

Includes index.
ISBN 978-1-55002-819-5

    1. Gould, Glenn, 1932-1982. 2. Pianists--Canada--Biography.
I. Title.

ML417.G69K82 2008   786.2092   C2008-900660-7

1 2 3 4 5   13 12 11 10 09

Conseil des Arts du Canada   Canada Council for the Arts   ONTARIO ARTS COUNCIL / CONSEIL DES ARTS DE L'ONTARIO

Canada

We acknowledge the support of the **Canada Council for the Arts** and the **Ontario Arts Council** for our publishing program. We also acknowledge the financial support of the **Government of Canada** through the **Book Publishing Industry Development Program** and **The Association for the Export of Canadian Books**, and the **Government of Ontario** through the **Ontario Book Publishers Tax Credit program**, and the **Ontario Media Development Corporation**.

Care has been taken to trace the ownership of copyright material used in this book. The author and the publisher welcome any information enabling them to rectify any references or credits in subsequent editions.

J. Kirk Howard, President

Printed and bound in Canada.
Printed on recycled paper.

www.dundurn.com

Dundurn Press	Gazelle Book Services Limited	Dundurn Press
3 Church Street, Suite 500	White Cross Mills	2250 Military Road
Toronto, Ontario, Canada	High Town, Lancaster, England	Tonawanda, NY
M5E 1M2	LA1 4XS	U.S.A. 14150

VLADIMIR KONIECCZNY

Glenn GOULD

A MUSICAL FORCE

DUNDURN PRESS
TORONTO

Contents

	Prologue: Controlled Energy	1
1	A Special Child	5
2	The Scourge of Lake Simcoe	15
3	Playing Like an Angel	27
4	In Love with the Microphone	39
5	On His Own Snowshoes	49
6	Becoming Glenn Gould	59
7	A Famous Concert Pianist	69
8	"That Nut's a Genius"	79
9	"Let's Ban Applause"	89
10	"Once I Let My Imagination Go …"	103
11	One of the God-People	113
	Epilogue: Elusive Voyager	125
	Chronology of Glenn Gould (1932–1982)	129
	Acknowledgements	155
	Sources Consulted	157
	Index	161

Glenn Gould at CBS photo session during recording of the Goldberg Variations, *New York, 1955. Courtesy of the Glenn Gould Estate.*

Prologue

On April 10, 1964, the Wilshire Ebell Theatre in Los Angeles is full. People whisper as they wait in anticipation for Glenn Gould, the eccentric young Canadian pianist who mesmerizes audiences with his unusual interpretations and bizarre stage mannerisms. Onstage are a magnificent black concert grand piano and a battered old folding chair that looks as if it won't support a hat safely, let alone a pianist. The chair is almost as famous as its owner, who is notorious for cancelling concerts at the last minute. During the past few years, Glenn has backed out of more performances than he has given, usually blaming one mysterious ailment or another.

Backstage, an attendant knocks on Glenn's dressing room door. "Ten minutes, Mr. Gould."

Glenn cocks his head. "Yes, thank you," he replies and turns back to the white basin in which he is soaking his hands and arms in hot water. Even after years of performing, he still finds that first knock unsettling. He looks at the wall clock as its red hand inexorably sweeps away the remaining time: six hundred, five hundred and fifty, four hundred and seventy seconds, and so on until the inevitable knock will come again and he will have to go onstage.

Feeling the heat penetrate deep into his bones, Glenn stares into the basin. After a few more minutes, he slowly lifts his hands out of the water, stands up and reaches for the white towel. His arms and hands are as pink from the heat as those of a newborn baby. The sensation of cool air on his skin soothes him. He flexes his fingers. Not a single tremor. Only half an hour earlier, his fingers had trembled like fidgety leaves. Now, nerves calmed by the tranquilizers he ingested an hour earlier, he is ready to play. "Miracles of science," he calls those little coloured capsules that he has been recommending to other musicians for years. Why fight stage fright when a few pills can make life so much easier?

He glances at the clock again, rolls down the sleeves of his loose white dress shirt and executes a few pirouettes, arms extended gracefully from his sides, the music he hears in his mind as loud and real as if he were playing it. A sharp knock breaks his reverie, and he knows it is time to go onstage. He puts on his dark blue suit jacket, runs a hand through his dishevelled blond hair, and looks in the mirror one last time before stepping out into the corridor. He takes his time walking toward the stage, his splay-footed gait slow but sure. He remembers a critic had once said that he walks like an impersonation of Henry Fonda impersonating Abe Lincoln.

He pauses for a moment and smoothes his jacket as an old memory flashes through his mind. A few years earlier, he had told his manager, Walter Homburger, that he would stop giving

A Musical Force

concerts when he turned thirty. Walter had stared at him in disbelief. Glenn resumes walking and shakes his head. He is now thirty-two and still putting himself through this ordeal. Sometimes, especially when he is playing a concerto with a symphony orchestra, he feels like a gladiator waiting for the crowd to signal thumbs up or thumbs down at the end of the performance. "I detest audiences," he whispers to himself as he finally reaches stage right.

Glenn pauses one last time and inhales deeply, his face serene, his blue eyes fixed on the piano. For this recital, he has chosen to play four fugues from *The Art of the Fugue*; the Partita in D Major also by J.S. Bach; Beethoven's Piano Sonata no. 30 in E Major, op. 109; and Hindemith's Sonata no. 3 in B-flat Major. Glenn had studied the intricate logic of Bach's music when he was a child, and he had discovered Hindemith at fifteen.

Eager to hear Canada's most famous pianist, and relieved that he hasn't cancelled this recital, the audience applauds generously as Glenn steps out from behind the curtain. Smiling shyly, he tips his head toward them and casts only the briefest of glances their way. Then he scrunches down onto the chair and immediately begins to move his lanky body this way and that as the seat creaks under his shifting weight. Once comfortable, he places his hands on the cool keyboard and waits a few seconds before stroking the keys. At the sound of the first note, he bends his head and shoulders forward until his nose hovers only inches above his hands.

As the voices of a Bach fugue spin out into the auditorium, the audience is hushed. A moment later, Glenn begins to hum and sing in out-of-tune accompaniment to the music. His body bobs, sways, circles, and dives over the keyboard while his slender fingers coax a clear, lovely tone from the nine-foot Steinway, every phrase perfectly etched. One hand occasionally strays away from the keys and drifts upward to conduct its partner through a complex passage.

Moved by the grace and beauty of Glenn's playing, the audience soon ignores his gestures and erratic humming. They watch his hands float above the keys, fingers pumping like little pistons, striking the keys with a minimum of movement yet producing beautiful round tones, each distinctly separate from the others with absolutely no blurring of sound and no reliance on the sustain pedal to glide through tortuous passages. The intense, controlled energy of Glenn's playing makes more than a few feet tap.

At the end of each piece, the crowd applauds enthusiastically, and Glenn, sweat dripping from his forehead, bows each time in acknowledgement. When the final note of the last composition sounds, he rises from the rickety old chair and leaves the stage, only to return immediately to thunderous applause. As he bows, an enigmatic smile plays across his face.

No one in the audience knows that this will be his last appearance. Glenn finally walks off the stage and returns to his dressing room to collect his assorted things. Even though it is April and warm in Los Angeles, he puts on his heavy overcoat and wraps a thick wool scarf around his neck. Then he tops off the ensemble with his trademark cap and leaves the theatre, folding chair in tow.

1

A Special Child

Bert Gould stared at the crib where his infant son lay dressed in a frilly white sleeper. A middle-aged man of medium height with a bushy moustache, steel-rimmed glasses, and neatly combed hair, Bert was a successful businessman who had never been heard to boast about anything, but he was extremely proud to be a new father. He and his wife, Florence, had waited years for this baby. Florence, especially, desperately longed for a son, but she had miscarried several times in the first years of their marriage. Fortunately, all went well this time, and on September 25, 1932, three years into the Great Depression, Glenn Herbert Gould was born. Like many babies in those days, he was born at home. Now, Florence, at the age of forty, was finally a mother.

As Bert continued watching his newborn son, he remembered the times during the previous nine months when Florence had played the piano and had sung, convinced her unborn infant

Glenn Gould at seven months old, 1933. Courtesy of the Glenn Gould Estate.

A Musical Force

could hear the glorious sounds of Bach, Mozart, Chopin, and her beloved church hymns even in the womb. From the first day of her pregnancy, she had been determined the baby would be a "special child." To her that meant one thing only — a musician.

In the early 1920s, several years before she met Bert, Florence had confided in a letter to a friend named Pearl that someday she would marry and have a boy named Glenn. Pearl replied the boy would probably be musical. With what must have been a twinkle in her eye, Florence wrote that she would see to that. To which Pearl had responded, "You were never satisfied with just anything, you wanted only the best."

Just then a sweet sound gently interrupted Bert's reverie. Astonished, he looked down at his son, who was humming and wiggling his fingers. Babies don't hum. They cry or scream when they're hungry or cranky, or gurgle and drool when they're happy, but they don't hum. When Bert later told the doctor how Glenn hummed and wiggled his fingers as if he were playing a keyboard, the doctor said, "This boy will be either a musician or a surgeon."

                ❦

Almost from the moment he was born, Glenn heard the sound of the piano, for Florence taught music and as soon as her son could sit upright, she took charge of his musical education. Every day, the two of them sat at the keyboard of the dark, gleaming upright piano, Glenn nestled like a kitten in her lap while she played Bach, Chopin, Mozart, and Haydn or sang hymns as her strong fingers drew thick, rich harmonies from the keyboard.

Bert frequently rested on the sofa watching the two of them. He possessed a fine voice and loved to sing in the church choir, and until he injured his hand, he also played the violin. Florence, however, was the driving musical force in the family, and he was content to stay in the background.

Warm and snug in his mother's embrace, Glenn listened to music, fascinated by the pattern of black and white keys, his whole being absorbed by the new sounds that touched his ears. One day, he stretched out his tiny arms, and Florence leaned in a little closer to the keyboard. One finger settled on an ivory key, smooth and cool to the touch. He depressed the key and listened intently to its vibrations until there was only silence. Then he repeated the action again and yet again.

Normally, children bang delightedly on the keys or smack them with open palms, crushing bunches of notes into a raucous sound. But even as an infant, Glenn never pounded the keys. "Glenn would always insist on pressing down a single key and holding it down until the resulting sound had completely died away," Bert said.

Glenn's parents weren't the only musicians in the family. Florence claimed to be a descendant of the Norwegian composer Edvard Grieg, although he had spelled his name slightly differently, with the *i* before the *e*. Bert's brothers were both amateur musicians, and Mary Greig, Glenn's maternal grandmother, played piano and organ. Sometimes the Goulds would drive to her house in Uxbridge, a small town near Toronto, where Glenn listened to Mary's reed organ. Piles of Victorian anthems and hymns were stacked on the instrument, and his grandmother cheerfully whipped through them for Glenn, her feet maniacally pumping the pedals, while her grandson sat still, lost in the hoarse, throaty sound that filled the carpeted living room.

Glenn was happy in his safe world. Several of his early photographs show a smiling cherub with wavy hair. In others, he is laughing and playing, never frowning or unhappy. For

A Musical Force

many other people, however, life was harsh during the 1930s. The Great Depression was in full force by the time Glenn was born. It had started with the stock market crash of October 1929 and continued unabated for the next ten years, ending only with the start of the Second World War. Thousands of businesses went bankrupt, and millions of North Americans lost their jobs and homes. People travelled by rail across the country, seeking employment no matter how menial. Men in Western Canada banded together and rode the rails in the famous On to Ottawa Trek of June 1935 to demand work. By the time they reached Regina, they were 1,800 strong. A riot broke out in that city and resulted in the death of one police officer. In all parts of the country, churches and charitable organizations were besieged with homeless people looking for a meal. "Brother, Can You Spare a Dime?" became the theme song of the Dirty Thirties, as the infamous decade came to be known.

Unlike many of their neighbours, the Goulds were fortunate because the Depression didn't affect them adversely. Bert worked every day at his firm, Gold Standard Furs, in downtown Toronto. He was in the business of selling fur coats and bartering animal skins, a lucrative but messy trade that provided the family with a comfortable income.

The Goulds lived in a modest two-storey brick house in Toronto's Beach area, which borders Lake Ontario. Like all the other houses on the block, theirs at 32 Southwood Drive had a small backyard and a manicured front lawn with a driveway to one side. A tall maple tree offered shade in the summer. Numerous winding, tree-lined streets criss-crossed the neighbourhood, and inviting parks provided places to picnic and play. People from all over the city packed the long sandy beach during the hot summers.

Glenn Gould

The Beach was a middle-class neighbourhood, its residents mostly White Anglo-Saxon Protestants like Florence and Bert, who were devout, highly principled, and proud of their heritage. Both worked hard and treated their friends kindly. The Goulds didn't flaunt their good fortune, nor did they show their emotions in public. Family, faith, work, discipline, and music — these were the cornerstones of their life. Members of the United Church, the family attended services regularly.

Florence traced her family roots back to a Scottish clan, the McGregors, who believed they were descended from Griogar, son of Alpin, King of the Scots in the eighth century. Bert's grandfather, Thomas, had been a Sunday school teacher and preacher. His family name was originally Gold, not Gould. Sometime around 1939, Bert and his father changed their name for reasons no one has ever understood, although some speculated that the family didn't want to be mistaken for being Jewish because in the Toronto of the 1930s, Jews were frequently harassed. Only Gentile Business Solicited and No Jews or Dogs Allowed were just two of the many crude signs posted by anti-Semites. This was a shameful period in Canadian history, one that deeply hurt all members of the Jewish community. To their credit, no one in Glenn's family was an anti-Semite.

For Glenn the world outside mattered very little. He had his mother, who devoted herself to him, and he had his music, which consumed his time. His ears devoured the simple songs Florence played for him. Those black dots strewn across cream-coloured paper attracted him, and he quickly made sense of the patterns they formed. By the time he was three, he could read music even though he couldn't yet read words. Many students struggle to memorize notes, relying on all kinds of mnemonic aids like Every Good Boy Deserves Favours and F-A-C-E to remember the names of the lines and space in the treble and bass clefs, but not Glenn. He intuitively understood the language of music the way other precocious children grasp the rules of chess.

One day, when he was three, Glenn surprised his father. Bert liked to spend time at his workbench in the basement and often took Glenn with him. A coloratura soprano was singing an opera aria on the radio. "Daddy, that's an A," Glenn said. Astounded, Bert took him upstairs immediately, sat him on the couch, walked over to the piano, and struck the same note. Glenn identified it instantly. Bert played another note. "B-flat," Glenn said, pleased with himself. Bert played several more notes, and Glenn named each one without looking. Bert realized that, like Mozart, his son had perfect pitch, and he was eager to share the discovery with Florence, for his wife believed that Glenn was very much like Mozart, whose extraordinary talent for music showed itself at about the same age.

Bert and Florence were elated. Perfect or absolute pitch is a rare gift possessed by perhaps only one in ten thousand people. Those who have it can identify any note or chord as easily as the rest of us can tell whether something is sweet or sour by taste, or recognize colours by sight. Mozart could instantly identify the pitch made by a watch or bell.

Now, Glenn received even more of Florence's attention, but even though he was her son, she disciplined him as strictly as she did all her students. She believed that singing helped to train the ear, so she encouraged all her pupils to sing the notes as they played them. Glenn, too, sang every note, and if his fingers slipped, she immediately corrected him. No matter where she was in the house, her ears were like radar, always attuned to her son's playing.

"No Glenn. That's C, not C-sharp. Please sit straight. Keep your fingers curled as if you're holding an orange in the palm of your hand." She refused to tolerate faking or sloppiness in his playing or posture and admonished him daily for any minor infraction. She was known to rap students' knuckles with a ruler for making mistakes. Sometimes, she forbade Glenn to play if he made too many errors. "That's enough. You're simply not concentrating," she might say and lock the piano lid. When this happened, Glenn was despondent, for this punishment was as unjust to him as not being allowed to go out to play hockey was for other boys.

Glenn longed to please his mother and tolerated her frequent criticisms. Initially, he obeyed her and did everything she said. His first book of music was *Keyboard Town* by Louise Robyn, and he whipped through it in no time at all. If he made a mistake, he repeated the passage slowly, then faster and faster until he played it perfectly and at the correct tempo. Mastering the notes made him feel good and impressed his mother, who never had to beg or bribe him to practise. As Glenn grew older, Florence and Bert had to set limits, otherwise Glenn would plop himself down at the piano and sit there all day, completely oblivious to the passage of time. Florence hounded him daily to go outside and play in the fresh air. At the same time, she would caution him about germs. If left to himself, Glenn ignored everything — household chores, games, and homework. Whenever there was anything to do that didn't involve music, Glenn vanished.

Once the Goulds realized that their son was a prodigy, they made every effort to ensure that he led a normal life, but they also understood that his talent couldn't remain hidden for long. As Glenn approached school age, the Goulds refused to let anyone use the word "prodigy" in their home. There have been many musical prodigies. Some, like the violinist Yehudi Menuhin, managed to have a productive lifelong career. Many others, however, burned out before they reached puberty. The most famous prodigy, Mozart, had been hosted by royalty yet died a pauper. Bert and Florence feared that Glenn, too, might be exploited by unscrupulous managers and greedy concert promoters. To protect their son, they limited his early exposure to the public.

When he was just five, Glenn performed for the Business Men's Bible Class in Uxbridge, Ontario. Florence and Bert sang a duet with Glenn as their accompanist. Glenn sight-read the music perfectly. Recently, he had also started composing his own songs, short pieces almost like rudimentary exercises in composition. The following day he played again and included two of his own tunes. The local paper praised him highly, claiming that "here was something of a musical genius in the making." Several months later, in December 1938, Glenn performed again, this time at the Emmanuel Presbyterian Church. Dressed in a white satin suit with short pants, he sat at the huge piano, his feet dangling from the bench. Much to his satisfaction, people paid him many compliments. Afterwards, he announced, "I am going to be a concert pianist."

Florence missed no opportunity to introduce Glenn to fine music. In 1938, the Polish-born pianist Josef Hofmann was giving a recital in Toronto's Massey Hall, an imposing brick structure with arched windows and superior acoustics. Glenn was six, and this would be his first visit to the famous hall. That evening, he sank into the soft balcony seat and waited expectantly. Presently, Hofmann, dressed in a black tuxedo, strode across the stage to the nine-foot concert grand. Placing his left hand on its frame, he bowed graciously then flicked the tails of his tuxedo back and up before sitting down on the bench. The audience hushed. Hofmann was a brilliant pianist, admired for his clear tone, magnetic stage presence, and astute intellect. He had been one of Europe's leading prodigies, gifted in composition, mathematics, science, and business. He was from that tradition of pianists often called Romantics. Like bravura pianists such as Vladimir Horowitz, Arthur Rubinstein, and Sergei Rachmaninov, Hofmann appealed to audiences as much for his hypnotic performances as for his musicianship. His repertoire included works by Chopin and Liszt, composers whose music demanded superb technique, which Hofmann had in abundance.

Hofmann's pianism enraptured Glenn. On the way home after the concert, he slumped in the back seat, tired but excited. He could hardly hear Florence saying, "Please sit up straight, Glenn. You'll ruin your posture if you continue to slouch." But Glenn, eyes glazed, drifted off into that delicious state between waking and sleeping where anything is possible. Then, from out of nowhere, glorious orchestral music filled his head, and he imagined that he, himself, was making every one of those sounds. Suddenly, he became Josef Hofmann. Glenn remembered that dream for the rest of his life.

2

The Scourge of Lake Simcoe

"Hey, jerk! You look like a real goof."

Glenn heard the insult, but kept walking, arms waving like wands as he conducted the music he heard in his mind.

"Goof!" The taunting voice was closer. "What a —"

Suddenly, Glenn whipped around and smacked Williamson Road Elementary School's worst bully. Shocked, the boy froze as Glenn grabbed him by the lapels and hissed, "If you ever come near me again, I'll kill you!"

Too stunned to reply, the bully wiggled and squirmed, desperate to free himself from Glenn's grip. "Let me go," he pleaded, but Glenn hung on to his tormentor for a few more seconds, then pushed him away and stomped off, so angry he felt as sick to his stomach as he had the first time he had visited his father's furrier business on Melinda Street in downtown Toronto

Glenn Gould and Florence Gould in front of the Lake Simcoe cottage, 1944. Courtesy of the Glenn Gould Estate.

and gasped at the sight of muskrat pelts strewn on the workroom floor. The repulsive sight and horrible stench of the still-bloody fur had nauseated Glenn. The poor creatures must have suffered terribly. For years after, whenever Florence wore a fur, Glenn chastened her. He once said, "By the time I was six, I'd already made an important discovery: that I get along much better with animals than with humans."

He walked faster and faster until he came to his front door. Once inside the house, he patted his dog, checked on his goldfish, then hurried to the waiting piano. As his fingers crab-walked along the keys, Glenn tried to make the instrument sound like the one he heard inside his head.

Much later, exhausted and sweaty, he went into the living room, where Florence sat in her favourite chair. He dropped to his knees beside his mother, and laid his head in her lap as he so often did. "That's a good boy," she whispered while she stroked his hair. Her gentle touch made him feel especially loved and safe.

In 1938, the year he was to begin Grade 1, Glenn harangued Bert and Florence until they hired a private tutor so their precious son wouldn't have to give up his idyllic existence to attend school. Years later he confessed, "When I was six, I managed to persuade my parents that mine was an uncommonly sensitive soul, which ought not to be exposed to the boorish vandalism I perceived among my contemporaries."

The tutor failed to work out and in September of 1939, Glenn enrolled in Williamson Road Elementary School, a typical three-storey red brick structure. Each day, he shuffled the block to school, sat in one of the wooden desks screwed to the floor in long rows, and counted the seconds to freedom. Perfectly executed letters of the alphabet loomed above the blackboard as reminders of the importance of good penmanship, a lesson that was completely lost on Glenn, whose handwriting was as sloppy as his piano technique was precise.

Even though Glenn skipped Grade 3, he disliked school, which he characterized as full of humourless teachers who taught tedious subjects and hostile students who relished picking on him. "I got along miserably with most of my teachers, and all of my fellow students," Glenn once admitted. As early as the second grade, he began to invent for excuses to stay home. During his first November at the public school, he was absent eleven and a half days.

Periods devoted to "organized relaxation" frustrated him the most. Twice each week, he endured instruction in vocal music as the teacher enthusiastically coerced the class to sing, "Pay attention, boys and girls. Breathe deeply. Make the vowels nice and round." Glenn purposefully entered at the wrong time in rounds like "Three Blind Mice" and "Frère Jacques," his nasally voice occasionally provoking the teacher to throw chalk at him. To Glenn, these classes were silly because they were so rudimentary compared with the ones he was taking at the Toronto Conservatory of Music, later the Royal Conservatory of Music, where he was winning silver medals for his piano examinations and studying organ with Frederick Silvester, under whose tutelage he was making rapid progress.

Recess wasn't much fun either. He usually leaned against the chain link fence alone with his thoughts while the other kids played tag or handball. His classmates teased and bullied him daily. "Hey chicken. Afraid of hurting your pinkies," some kid would call out and heave a ball straight at him. But Glenn

A Musical Force

ignored the taunts and jammed his hands even deeper into his pockets. He refused to risk his hands on something as stupid as playing ball.

In Grade 4, Glenn met Robert Fulford, who was as smart and curious as he was, and the two of them spent hours together. They hooked up tin cans to string and telegraphed secret messages between their yards, or they listened to CBC Radio, heads bent toward the speaker, their attention riveted by reports from the war front, for the Second World War raged during almost their entire time in elementary school. Everyone experienced food and gas rationing. Air raid sirens howled periodically, and neighbourhood lights dimmed or blacked out completely. Until the war ended in 1945, the year he completed Grade 8, Glenn, together with Robert, sat glued to the radio night after night completely absorbed by the graphic descriptions of horrible battles like the one at Dieppe where the Nazis slaughtered nine hundred Canadian soldiers in just a few hours.

When he wasn't mastering scales and pieces or engaged in heated debates about global issues with his friend, Glenn pored over maps of the North and read voraciously, especially stories about explorers. He developed a deep love of words, always using two when one would do, and even published his own newspaper, *The Daily Woof*, in which he reported on his many pets. He owned goldfish named Bach, Beethoven, Chopin, and Haydn, and a budgie named Mozart, which perched on the piano while he played. A dog, Sir Nicholas of Garloscheed, or "Nicky," was his constant companion. One summer, Glenn even befriended a skunk that had been rooting around in the garbage at the cottage.

Glenn spent most of his time at home, where he felt safe and secure. At school, he fretted about germs. If someone sneezed or coughed, he covered his face. One morning, the classroom erupted in laughter as a boy vomited on the floor. Glenn felt powerless and panicky. He shuddered, terrified he might throw up, too. He dashed home at noon, armed himself with two soda mints to reduce stomach acid, and brought them to class just in case he became ill. He would make sure that no one was going to stare at him. A few days later, he brought stronger medication: aspirin. Still, the fear of embarrassing himself was unbearable.

Florence, who was a "bit of a dragon" according to Robert, only made matters worse. She nagged Glenn daily to get more exercise and at the first sign of a cough or sniffle, she ordered him to bed. Often, just as he was about to step out the door, she warned him about the dangers outside. "Please be careful. Stay away from people who are coughing. There are germs everywhere." She even refused to let Glenn attend the Canadian National Exhibition because he might be exposed to all kinds of germs at the fairgrounds.

✦

In class, Glenn daydreamed about the family cottage at Uptergrove on the shores of Lake Simcoe near Orillia, Ontario, a place Stephen Leacock had immortalized in his *Sunshine Sketches of a Little Town*. A simple structure painted white with green trim, the cottage looked out over the lake. Maple and birch trees dotted the property, their cool green leaves turning into rich reds, yellows and browns every fall.

At the cottage, Glenn practised whenever he liked and played with Ray Dudley and Clarence Little, who were neighbours. Clarence's mother once said Glenn "seemed happiest when he was practising the piano." Others thought him "a solitary child with strong opinions." The owner of the local store saved crumpled

A Musical Force

dollar bills that fell out of Glenn's pocket on his solitary walks and returned them to his young customer when he came by to purchase something.

The Goulds had their own dock and Bert installed a rail so Glenn could ease his boat into the lake. One summer day when Glenn was ten, he and a few friends decided to take the boat out. They piled into the small craft while it was still on the rail. Glenn lowered himself onto the back seat. Without warning, the boat started to slide down the rail. Alarmed, Glenn jumped up and spilled backwards out of the boat. He dropped straight down and hit his spine on the jagged rocks a meter or so below. He lay winded and wincing with pain as his friends hovered over him. The next day, he was still sore. Throughout that entire summer, and for months afterwards, he complained of pain, but doctors could not find anything seriously wrong.

Despite the pain, the next morning Glenn bundled himself up in a coat, hat, and scarf even though it was summer and set off on a hike through the countryside, his beloved dog Nicky by his side. They ambled down a dusty path and through a thick stand of trees. He threw his head back and began to sing while his arms waved like those of a mad conductor. Nicky panted beside him. Glenn stopped for a moment and looked out between some birch trees. The lake was a muted silvery-grey today. He could hear birds chirping. The air was still and warm. There were no school bullies here ready to make his life miserable. He resumed his walk and shortly his long arms began again to weave arcs in the air as he conducted an imaginary orchestra. Later that afternoon, he got on his bike and pedalled for miles, stopping only to serenade a herd of grazing cows, his once lovely boy soprano now a "squawk," according to Bert.

The wooden boat skimmed the calm surface of Lake Simcoe, its shadow reflected in the glassy water. The two men aboard squinted their eyes in the morning sun as they searched for the weed bed hidden just a few feet below the surface. A slight breeze brushed the lake, creating wavelets as tight and shiny as fish scales.

"Drop 'er, here, the older man said, pointing a gnarled finger toward the water. "Pike'll be hiding in those weeds for sure."

They shut off the ten-horse outboard motor and dropped the anchor, a battered paint can filled with cement. Both men grabbed their rods and began setting hooks into the mouths of sucker minnows. They cast their lines and the minnows plopped into the water and disappeared. Only two red and white floats bobbed on the surface.

A few minutes later, a cedar runabout appeared with Glenn at the wheel and Nicky beside him. Glenn bore down on the floats. The two anglers stared in disbelief as they watched him zoom by their floats. "Beat it, you idiot. You'll scare off the fish!" one yelled.

Glenn laughed. That was exactly what he intended to do. He turned the boat and swooped by the bobbers again. He hated fishing. Once, when he was six, he had gone out on the lake with a neighbour and his son. When they found a good spot by some reeds, the man said, "Drop your lines, boys." A moment later, Glenn felt an inquisitive tug on his rod and yanked it hard. Up came a perch, wiggling on the hook. Shocked, Glenn gaped at the little yellow fish with black stripes. In that instant, he knew how that poor fish felt. He jumped up and screamed in protest. The boat rocked from side to side and the man yelled, "Sit down right now," and shoved him back on to the seat. Glenn vowed

A Musical Force

to never fish again and hounded Bert until he, too, gave up the sport. Glenn called himself the Scourge of Lake Simcoe, and plenty of fishers called him worse names than that.

Glenn's boating excursions often caused Bert and Florence hours of worry because the weather could change quickly, and even a slow wind could blow up good-sized waves. One Saturday afternoon, Glenn cruised out to annoy anglers. Engrossed in his hunt, he didn't notice the clouds rolling in until he was about a half-mile from shore. The wind picked up, the sky darkened, and fat drops of rain bubbled the lake's surface. A few minutes later, whitecaps pitched the boat to and fro. Glenn noticed that the waves had a certain rhythm to them. He braced himself against the seat and began to conduct them as if they were a huge watery orchestra. Florence grew worried and sent Bert out to find him. As Bert pulled alongside Glenn's boat, he saw his son waving his arms and singing, completely indifferent to the danger. Father and son returned home soaking wet.

That night Glenn dreamt that all the rocks around the lake were covered with dead leaves. He dreaded leaving the cottage, and often had the same dream when it was time to leave. He remained silent all the way home. Later, he attended evening service with his parents. In the stillness of the church, its stained glass windows glowing in the late afternoon sun, he lost himself in the inspiring harmonies of familiar hymns sung by the church choir and accompanied by the haunting sounds of the organ.

※

By 1943, Glenn had already captured the attention of Toronto's tight musical community. With Florence as his teacher he had made rapid progress, and by the age of ten he could play every piece

23

Glenn Gould

in Book One of *The Well-Tempered Clavier* by J.S. Bach. Glenn was awarded the Silver Medal for Grade 3 piano. In fact, he earned first-class honours in all his piano examinations. He had started organ lessons with Frederic K. Silvester a year earlier in 1942, and had discovered that organ studies improved his piano technique and also taught him the importance of the bass line in music. He liked to tell people that by playing the organ he learned to "think with his feet." During this time, he also studied theory with Leo Smith. Although Glenn's marks in counterpoint and form weren't outstanding, he admired the way a composer like Bach could so ingeniously weave together several different musical lines.

In 1943, Florence found her son a new piano teacher, someone who would nurture his unique talents. She engaged Alberto Guerrero, a Chilean-born concert pianist who had immigrated to Canada in the 1920s and was teaching for the Toronto Conservatory of Music. An avuncular man in his mid-fifties and a stern taskmaster who counted among his many friends such world-renowned pianists as Claudio Arrau, Guerrero sensed that Glenn was like a high-spirited colt that needed lots of free rein. Guerrero knew instinctively that Glenn couldn't be ordered to do anything; rather, he had to be pointed in a direction and allowed to explore it for himself. Even at that age, Glenn "had a perfectly good idea of his powers," according to Guerrero. With Guerrero's guidance, Glenn's reputation grew. The musical community in the Toronto of the 1940s was small, and word quickly spread about the "boy wonder" who in February of 1944 won first prize at the First Annual Kiwanis Music Festival.

Anyone who has ever entered a music competition knows about being nervous. Students spend months perfecting one piece, which they have to play from memory. They worry about

A Musical Force

making mistakes or about forgetting the music completely. Finally, the dreaded day arrives. The hall is full of parents praying silently that their child will win. The adjudicator sits at a small table, sharpened pencil in hand, while the competitors sit at the front of the auditorium waiting their turn. The room hums with conversation between performances as parents and friends whisper their criticisms. What do the young contestants think and feel? Some hope that other competitors will make lots of mistakes. Others probably wish they had never taken piano lessons. A few are eager to show off their talent. For all of them, it's a tense time: palms sweat, hands tremble, and stomachs flutter.

This was Glenn's first Kiwanis competition. The other contestants were older; several of them were highly skilled young musicians. Glenn, who was not quite twelve, wore short pants onstage and fidgeted a bit before he played. Perhaps he, too, was nervous, especially in this company, but from the first note to the last, he held everyone's attention. A reporter wrote that Glenn had "that sort of commanding intelligence and responsibility which indicate ability worth watching." Glenn was thrilled with the praise.

The next year, 1945, Glenn played on the radio for the first time in a program airing the winners of the festival, and he was awarded the Gordon Thompson Scholarship at the Kiwanis Music Festival. Passing his piano exam for the Toronto Conservatory of Music (now the Royal Conservatory of Music) Associateship that June made him especially proud, for he was the youngest student ever to earn the coveted diploma.

A week before Christmas Day of 1945, Glenn gave his first formal public recital in Eaton Auditorium in downtown Toronto. He played the huge Casavant organ, whose sounds ranged from whispery flutes to impossibly deep, grumbling basses. His friend

Robert sat on the bench and turned the pages of the music while Glenn took command of the organ's manuals. One reviewer wrote, "A genius he is, with the modesty that only true genius knows… From start to finish and in every detail his playing had the fearless authority and finesse of a master." The review made Glenn very happy.

3

Playing Like an Angel

Glenn sat at the kitchen table watching his mother water the African violets on the windowsill. His cousin Jessie Greig had come to stay with them while she attended Teachers' College. At twenty-one, she was six years older than he. Jessie was like a sister to him although he called her "meddlin' country cuzzin" and teased her mercilessly.

A few weeks earlier, after Jessie had just finished waxing the kitchen floor, Glenn deliberately upended a glass of water on it. She chased him around the house until she caught him and rubbed his face with a filthy cloth.

"I'll wring your neck," he screamed, running after her as she dashed to her bedroom and slammed the door, refusing to come out. So he grabbed her notebook and tore it up page by page.

"I'll fail. I'll fail," she cried through the door.

"That's good," he replied, "If I studied as much as you, I'd

MASSEY HALL
Season
1946 - 1947

Secondary School Concert

The Toronto Symphony Orchestra

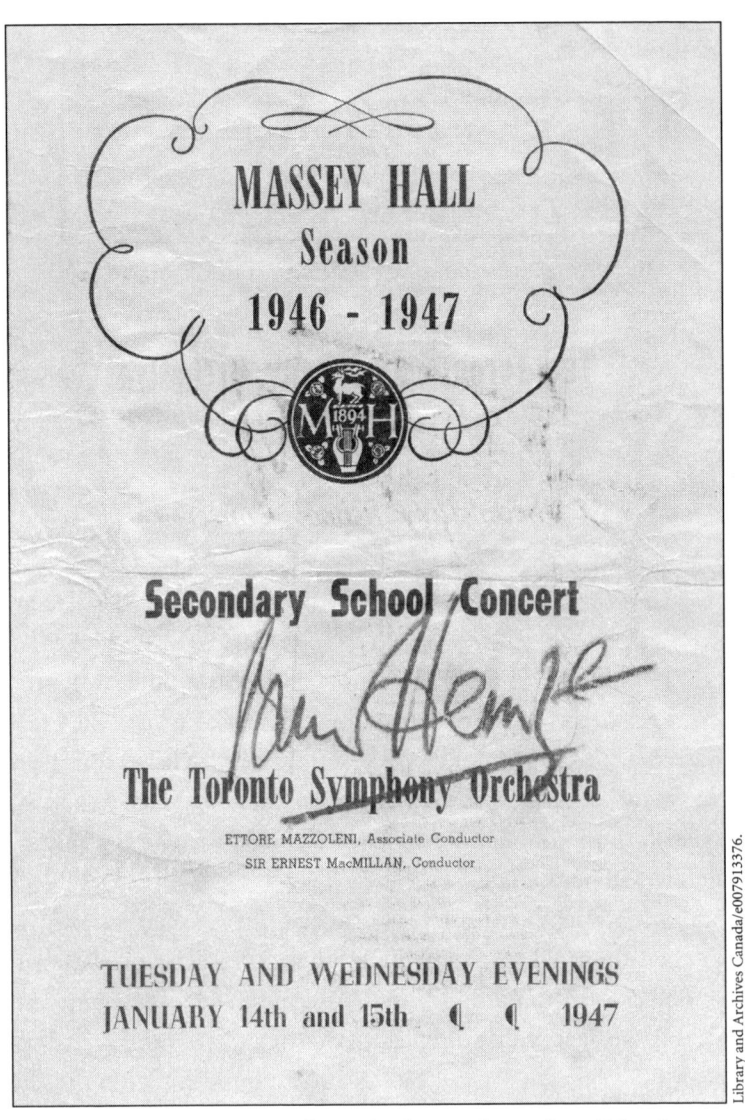

ETTORE MAZZOLENI, Associate Conductor
SIR ERNEST MacMILLAN, Conductor

TUESDAY AND WEDNESDAY EVENINGS
JANUARY 14th and 15th 1947

Program for Toronto Symphony Orchestra Secondary School Concert at Massey Hall, Toronto, January 14–15, 1947. The cover is autographed by guest conductor, Bernard Heinze. Courtesy of the Glenn Gould Estate.

A Musical Force

be finished university by now." He meant it, too. Of course, they forgave each other quickly.

Glenn glanced slyly at his mother as she finished watering the plants. She was so easy to fluster. "Caruso is a clown, he's terrible, awful, horrible, a fraud, exactly what music shouldn't be," he said, dismissing in one sentence a singer many considered to be the world's greatest operatic tenor of his generation. Florence treasured the Italian's 78 rpm records.

"Oh, Glenn, you mustn't say things like that," Florence replied, exasperated yet again by her brilliant, opinionated son. "Caruso was a great singer. You don't know anything about it. You've only listened to a few records he's made, and they're scratchy. How can you judge him on that?" But Glenn had made up his mind about the great Italian tenor: too dramatic for his taste. Music should be reserved, elegant, and intellectually demanding, everything that opera and Caruso were not.

Glenn shrugged and stood up as Jessie looked at him, admiring her lanky cousin with his blond uncombed hair and kind eyes. It was 1946 and Glenn was fifteen, almost sixteen. Glenn laughed and headed for the special practice room Bert had built for him.

Once inside, Glenn picked up the score of Beethoven's Piano Concerto no. 4 in G Major, op. 58, which he was to perform with the Toronto Conservatory Orchestra in just a few weeks, and studied the music for a few minutes. He slid off the chair, knelt down beside a tall stack of 78 rpm records, and sorted through them until he found Arthur Schnabel's recording of the concerto. Glenn admired Schnabel, who was also a writer and intellectual. During the past few years, Glenn had heard several of the world's leading pianists like Arthur Rubinstein, Claudio Arrau, and Vladimir Horowitz, but Schnabel was still his hero.

When Schnabel was a young man, his teacher had said to him, "You'll never be a pianist; you are a musician." Glenn understood that remark: Music wasn't simply about what instrument you played. First and foremost, true musicians were artists.

Glenn placed the first of the four well-worn discs on the turntable, sat at the keyboard, leaned over, and dropped the needle on the record. As the opening notes sounded, he closed his eyes and listened intently. Exactly four minutes and twenty-eight seconds later, the record slowed to a halt, and Glenn quickly flipped it over. In those days, long-playing recordings hadn't been invented yet, so lengthy pieces often took both sides of the disc and sometimes several discs. This concerto took eight full sides, and Glenn listened to them all.

Then he put the first disc on the turntable again. His fingers dug into the keys, and as he bobbed and swayed along with the master, he imagined himself onstage accompanied by a full symphony orchestra. A while ago, Guerrero had learned of Glenn's attempts at imitation and was not amused. "Please stop listening to the Schnabel recordings," his teacher had implored, threatening also to take them from Glenn. But Schnabel's interpretation, technique, and fat, robust tone were too appealing. Glenn did not acquiesce to his teacher's demands. Now, awash in the gorgeous double sound of the record and his own playing, Glenn fantasized he was Schnabel himself.

Afterwards, as he scanned a particularly finicky passage in the first movement, Glenn placed his right hand over the keys corresponding to the printed notes, and with his left index finger, he tapped each finger precisely. As each one dropped and lifted like a smooth piston, Glenn sighed contentedly, his mind calmed by the soothing repetitiveness of the finger-tapping technique that Guerrero had shown him.

A Musical Force

Tired of tapping, Glenn turned his radio on full blast. Listening to loud music or any sustained noise while playing helped him learn. He had made that discovery one day while he was working on Mozart's Fugue in C Major, K. 394, and the Goulds' maid came into the room dragging the vacuum cleaner behind her. Usually, Glenn argued with her whenever she intruded, but this time he ignored her. The instant she turned the vacuum on, the loud whining blocked the music out completely like the white noise in a dentist's office. But as Glenn played on, he could feel Mozart's fugue with his fingers even though he couldn't hear a note. The sensation was peculiar, but it helped him to understand music's structure better.

From then on, he used noise as a way to analyse music or to help him master difficult fingering. Unable to hear the actual sound of the piano, he could focus completely on the tactile sensation of his fingers walking across the keys while he imagined the sounds they were making. He was overwhelmed and energized by this insight. Perhaps this was the beginning of his future dissatisfaction with any piano he played, for no instrument could reproduce faithfully that exquisite quality of tone he heard in his mind.

Finally, exhausted and hungry, Glenn turned off the radio, lowered his head, and mentally replayed the music he had just practised. He had been cooped up in his room for nearly five hours. When he was younger, his parents had a rule: a maximum of four hours practice time each day. Bert occasionally had to speak gruffly to Glenn. "I will lock up the piano if you don't obey," he had told him on more than one occasion. But after a few years, he, too, had given up because Glenn protested so much.

On May 8, 1946, Glenn performed the first movement of Beethoven's Piano Concerto no. 4 in G Major with the Toronto

Conservatory Orchestra. Glenn thought, *This is a time for personal statement — a moment to grasp and to make my own.* So he walked across the stage to the piano, sat down, and played the way he wanted to, occasionally pushing back his hair or dabbing his face with a white handkerchief, all the while bending low over the keyboard, his rounded shoulders like those of a much older man.

Guerrero was angry and hurt at having his wishes completely ignored. Glenn left in high spirits, but his teacher was shattered. The press, on the whole, were quite kind. According to Glenn, one critic asked, "Who does the kid think he is, Schnabel?" No record of that supposed comment has ever been found.

One man who sat in the audience that evening was "bowled over" by Glenn's artistry. Walter Homburger approached Bert and Florence with an offer to manage their son. "I thought the concert was phenomenal," he said. Walter had recently immigrated to Canada from Germany and aspired to become an impresario who promoted talented musicians. Homburger was twenty-two, only eight years older than Glenn, and like Glenn, he was inexperienced, but determined.

❦

"B-minus, Mr. Gould," the English teacher said as he handed back Glenn's essay entitled, "My Plans for the School Year." Glenn smirked, took the paper, and flipped through it. The teacher had written, "That cannot be" and "Clever" in bold red ink. A few days earlier, Glenn, with his usual flair, had penned a wordy piece, that contained the cocky statement, "My plans for the school year, therefore, are non-existent." Satisfied, he had dropped the black pen on his desk, leaned back in the chair, and read over the entire essay. Of course, he had plans, many of them, but they involved

A Musical Force

only music. He jammed the essay into his binder and waited impatiently for the bell to ring. He had things to do.

By January 1947, Glenn was ready for his debut with the Toronto Symphony Orchestra. On January 14, he sat on the same stage from which Josef Hofmann had mesmerized him almost ten years earlier. This time, Glenn played the entire Piano Concerto no. 4 in G Major, op. 58 by Beethoven under the baton of Australian conductor Bernard Heinze.

Surrounded by ninety of the finest musicians in Canada, Glenn waited for the downbeat, his eyes focused on the keys of the Steinway grand. As soon as he struck the first notes, he forgot about the hundreds of watching eyes. After a few minutes, he began to brush his pant legs whenever he had a few bars rest. The audience wondered what he was doing, but applauded enthusiastically. When the closing chords died away, a reviewer in the *Toronto Daily Star* wrote, "Every inch a boy, he sat waiting for his cues to come in as though he'd have enjoyed a whiz-bang at cops and robbers." The *Evening Telegram* said, "He played Beethoven like a master."

Glenn was a little put off because one reviewer had drawn attention to his quirky behaviour, which had caused a few missed entrances in the *tutti* sections. Never at a loss for words, Glenn offered an explanation: "As I was getting into my best dark suit, my father cautioned me to keep my distance from Nick, but that, of course, was easier said than done. Nick was an affectionate and concerned animal and not one to see a friend off on an important mission without offering his good wishes." In short, Glenn was covered in dog hair, which he had noticed during a pause in the slow movement, and naturally he had tried to brush it off.

With his symphony debut behind him, Glenn entered a new phase in his career, and 1947 was shaping up to be one of the most significant years in his young life. He was ready to give full public recitals and eagerly anticipated the future.

The first concert, billed as Glenn Gould from the Studio of Alberto Guerrero, took place on April 10 at the Toronto Conservatory of Music. Glenn disarmingly described his programme as "a brace of fugues and some Haydn, some Beethoven, some Mendelssohn, some Liszt." On that day, he stepped up to the piano eagerly and hardly felt himself sit down. The butterflies tickling his stomach subsided as soon as his fingers touched the keys. Over the next hour, he easily navigated the contrapuntal intricacies of Bach, confidently outlined the theme in Beethoven's sonata, and played Chopin as if he were composing the piece himself on the spot. The *Globe and Mail* ran the headline "Gould Displays Growing Artistry."

Shortly after, Glenn appeared in various venues around Toronto, including Simpson's department store, where he followed a puppet show called Tubby the Tuba, and at the exclusive Empire Club in the Royal York Hotel. On occasion, he ventured out of the city to play in towns like Newmarket, Ontario. His reputation grew with each appearance and new fans talked about the peculiar teenager who spoke like a professor and played like an angel.

Walter Homburger arranged to have him take part in the International Artists Series at Eaton Auditorium on October 20, 1947. Glenn posed for glossy black and white publicity photos. His smooth, handsome face appeared on announcements and in the programmes. He couldn't wait to play Scarlatti, Beethoven, Couperin, Chopin, Liszt, and Mendelssohn. When he received the nod to go on, Glenn ambled across the stage with his loose-legged, loping walk, his five-foot eleven-inch frame slightly stooped. He sat down without noticing how few people were in attendance and began to sway in time to the music, the flowing lines accented by grunting and singing.

One reviewer gushed, "He stupefied the audience, especially men. Spider-like fingers, flexible rubber wrists, pedal infallible, nose a foot above the keys, he was an old man on a music spree… he outdid Rachmaninov for intensely supple art." Another called Glenn's playing "uncanny." Glenn's friend Ray Dudley said his pal's playing was "polished and poetic."

❧

Since the fall of 1945, Glenn had been attending Malvern Collegiate Institute. Although he found secondary school more tolerable than elementary school, he still resented having to spend time at school, even though he attended classes only in the mornings and devoted the rest of the day to his to organ, piano, and theory studies. When the mood struck him, he outperformed everyone in his class. Whizzing through Euclid's propositions, which were like the puzzles he enjoyed solving at home, he had completed Grade 10 Geometry in less than two months. English Literature was another favourite subject. In History, he soaked up tales about adventurers and explorers. Still, he couldn't read or discuss only what he liked, but was expected to answer difficult questions in all school subjects. What was the effect of the Concordat of 1801? What was the effect of the American Civil War on the development of the Canadian West? What is the difference between a Petrarchan and a Shakespearean sonnet?

If a subject piqued Glenn's curiosity, he dedicated himself to developing complete answers. He filled his notebooks with page after page of illegible handwriting on subjects like Jane Austen's *Pride and Prejudice* and anything to do with Canadian history. He earned satisfactory but not outstanding marks: French between 50 and 60 percent; English 70s to low 80s. But he also had a weakness for purple prose. One of his essays began: "Far down, through the concrete channel, a myriad of flustered flotsam floundered against a flurry of the wind squall. From far up, I saw a vacillating abstract of surrealistic shape whose very minute movements only multiplied my misconception of their unity." Well before the teacher read the last word of this particular composition, his eyes had glazed over. In other essays, Glenn's youthful pomposity showed itself in ponderous phrases like "pet antipathy," "contemporary thought," and "firm resolution to resist conversion."

Sometimes teachers' criticisms were quite blunt and cutting. "Just stuff and nonsense," one instructor wrote. Another, in responding to Glenn's essay on *Macbeth*, said that most of the paper was a "waste of words." The annoyed man had also added, "You are absent too often and miss too much work. Your knowledge is not thorough, nor your application of it sufficiently exact."

Bert, puzzled by the low grade on one essay, paid the instructor a visit only to be told, "Mr. Gould, I am a busy teacher and have better things to do with my time than to read papers that require one to constantly have to refer to a dictionary for half of the words used."

The other students at Malvern understood that Glenn was brilliant if a bit eccentric, and they accepted him. One boy, Wayne Fulford, said, "Already we knew he was special. He knew it, too." Glenn's peers dubbed him the "Ten Hottest Fingers at Malvern," and he, in turn, entertained them at a variety of school functions. For one school assembly, Glenn arranged Beethoven's "Emperor" Concerto so his friend Ray Dudley could play it on piano while he, himself, played the orchestral part on organ. Two years later, in 1949, Glenn revealed his talent for composing with a suite of his own music, which he played as an overture to the school's production of *Twelfth Night*.

Glenn was always relaxed and in control in front of a microphone. A photo from a 1955 recording session is visible on monitors in the background. Courtesy of the Glenn Gould Estate.

4

In Love with the Microphone

"Oh, it's all right, Glenn," Alberto Guerrero said, peering at his hunched-over student through rimless glasses. "You've played those bars perfectly the last five times. That's enough for now."

Without looking up at his balding teacher, Glenn retorted, "No, it's not."

Not surprised, Guerrero sat patiently in his chair. From the time he had first met Glenn five years earlier, the middle-aged Chilean had sensed the young pianist's determination to do things his own way. After one three-hour session with his gifted pupil, Guerrero said to his wife, Myrtle, "The whole secret of teaching Glenn is to let him discover things for himself."

Now, Guerrero watched Glenn attack the passage again and again in his search for a different nuance of tone or shift in phrasing. Glenn's technique was becoming crisp and clean. His long, thin fingers articulated each key with economical precision, and the separation between notes was absolutely distinct. The effect was a clear and delicate tone.

Playing the piano at the concert level is extremely strenuous. A major concerto can exhaust a pianist's physical and mental powers. In preparation, students devote years to mastering countless scales and diabolically difficult études. Technique, however, involves much more than the rapid movement of one's fingers. The whole body is involved, and Guerrero had definite ideas about the mechanics of piano playing. One student, John Beckwith, said of Guerrero, "As a teacher, he had exceptional resources, but no method."

Guerrero encouraged Glenn to sit lower and occasionally pressed down on his shoulders so Glenn could press up against the weight to develop strong back muscles. Sometimes, Glenn collapsed under the pressure. One time, Guerrero persuaded Glenn, who loathed physical exertion, to help Bert saw firewood as an exercise for his hands and arms.

Over the years, Guerrero introduced Glenn and other students to the finger-tapping technique as well as to unique exercises not found in any method book. "Pretend you are catching a fly with one hand," he suggested one day. At another lesson, he said, "Rotate your wrists and elbows but keep the hands loose." And still another time, he said, "Play scales legato with only one finger, using only your upper arm to move the finger." Guerrero also advised Glenn to keep his arms level with the keyboard and to let his fingers lie flatter on the keys for improved facility. "Glenn won't take anyone's word for anything," Guerrero once said, so he never ordered; instead, he let the teenager experiment for himself.

Now, as he listened to Glenn repeat the passage interminably, Guerrero felt proud of the great progress his gifted pupil had

A Musical Force

made. After a few more minutes, Guerrero said, "Enough, Glenn. It's good, very, very good."

Glenn, forehead damp from effort, looked up. "Yes, but the trill could be crisper," and with the middle and index fingers of his right hand fluttering like a hummingbird's wings, he trilled G to F-sharp and winced at the piano's inadequacy to reproduce the light, ringing sound he heard in his mind.

No piano satisfied Glenn's ears. Over the past five years or so, Bert had had bought several instruments and spent at least $3,000 annually on lessons, which in the 1940s was enough money to support an entire family for a year. At first, Bert purchased upright pianos, but Glenn soon demanded grands. The cottage, too, needed a new piano every year or so because summer humidity and winter cold split sound boards and warped pin blocks. Bert loved Glenn, and was happy to indulge him, but he finally drew the line when Glenn asked him to tear out a wall in the house to install an organ.

Glenn finished off the trill with a flourish and stood up ready to leave, but Guerrero said, "I'd like to play something for you."

Glenn sat in the chair while his teacher placed some music on the stand and began to play. The music sounded thorny to Glenn's ears; its intervals were unusual and dissonant. Alberto then played a second piece, obviously by the same composer, for the music again sounded discordant and alien. Guerrero finished the piece and looked at Glenn slouching in the chair with his long legs crossed and hands cupped behind his head.

"These pieces, Opus 11 and Opus 19, are by Arnold Schoenberg," Guerrero said. Glenn shook his head, signalling his rejection of the two compositions. Guerrero protested, but Glenn imperiously dismissed his comments, much as he had one day when the two of them had discussed Mozart, whose music the

Chilean loved. As a boy, Guerrero had lain awake at night greedily eavesdropping as adults played four-hand arrangements of the young genius's Symphony no. 40 in G Minor. Glenn scorned this work and once said this symphony, "has eight remarkable measures... surrounded by a half hour of banality."

The day's lesson ended, Glenn said goodbye and left for home. A few weeks later, he arrived at his lesson at Guerrero's home with a few short pieces he had composed in a style similar to Schoenberg's.

⁂

The two pieces Guerrero had played that day in 1948 were not the first modern compositions Glenn had heard. Approximately one year earlier, he had turned on his radio one evening just in time to catch a few words about Paul Hindemith and his composition *Matthias the Painter*. During the moment's silence before the music started, he flopped into his chair and waited. He wasn't expecting much. Hindemith was a major composer of the first half of the twentieth century. Glenn claimed that his taste in music didn't extend much beyond Richard Wagner.

When the first notes of *Matthias the Painter* filled the room, Glenn sat up, reached over and turned up the volume. His face grew slack and his eyes gazed at some distant spot. A few minutes later, Florence entered his room, saw him sitting transfixed, and immediately left.

When the recording ended, he sighed, then jumped up and began to pace. The music continued to play over and over in his mind. This was something new, a recreation of a certain kind of Baroque temperament that moved him deeply. He felt exhilarated. At fifteen, he had come alive to contemporary music.

A Musical Force

Until this point, Glenn had favoured Baroque and Classical composers, with some Romantics like Chopin, Liszt, and Mendelssohn mixed in. Now, inspired after hearing Hindemith and then Schoenberg, Glenn immersed himself in contemporary compositional technique and searched out many books on the subject. Serial, or twelve-tone music, especially, captured his imagination because it was like mathematics: organized, logical, and precise. Here was something much like his beloved fugues, and he couldn't get enough of Schoenberg and two men who had been his pupils: Anton Webern and Alban Berg. Glenn had found a soapbox, and he would spend years trying to convince people of this music's strange beauty.

When he was older, Glenn said that he became interested in modern music because "some of his teachers hated it." Maybe a few of them did, for contemporary compositions, and especially Schoenberg's, were not well received in the Toronto of the 1940s and 1950s. Guerrero, however, was thoroughly familiar with this music and introduced it not only to Glenn but to Toronto's musical community.

Arnold Schoenberg's music, especially the compositions of his middle period, was rejected by many concert-goers. Midway through his career, Schoenberg had developed a radical method of composition called the twelve-tone system, formally known as dodecaphonic technique, a word Glenn added to his vocabulary immediately. This is complex, unusual music. It is atonal music, which means it has no key centre as, for example, a Mozart sonata has. Most audiences are used to music that follows well-established rules of harmony and composition, but Schoenberg's serial pieces adhered to their own rules and were avant-garde and highly controversial as a result.

Imagine watching a television show. The actors speak English

43

but string the syllables together in unexpected ways. You don't understand any of the words even though you recognize the sounds as English. You know this is a television show, and you recognize its format or structure. It's both familiar and strangely foreign at the same time. When the show is over, you know you've seen a television show, but you can't really say much about what happened. That's how serial music seems to many who hear it.

Yet even though written in the early twentieth century, this music reminded Glenn of his other great loves — Renaissance, Classical, and especially Baroque music with its intricate counterpoint etchings. Like twelve-tone technique, counterpoint is also devilishly difficult. It uses many voices and follows strict rules. Composers need great intellect to master counterpoint and to weave all the threads into a satisfactory whole. Composing a fugue, for example, requires the kind of mind possessed by great chess masters, a mind that can recognize complex patterns and see many moves ahead. Glenn had such a mind, and could keep track of many different things at once. When he played, he often thought about other things. During a conversation or argument, he might be analyzing a musical score in his head or drafting his next essay.

At the moment, however, Glenn also faced a dilemma. He was pulled in two directions. On the one hand, he was loyal to composers like Orlando Gibbons, Bach, and Haydn. On the other hand, Hindemith, Schoenberg, Webern, and Berg tugged at him. Something had to give, so he cast off the Romantics like Chopin, even though he played the Polish composer's haunting music beautifully. One of Robert Fulford's most pleasant memories as a teenager was to listen to Glenn's interpretations of Chopin drift off into the warm summer night. The Canadian composer Oskar Morawetz heard Glenn soulfully play a Chopin nocturne, yet claim to like only composers up to the time of Beethoven. Glenn said of Chopin, in particular, that he wrote only short pieces, didn't know how to develop his ideas, and demanded too much use of the pedal for colouration.

Even as a teenager, Glenn was a puritan at heart. Profoundly influenced by his parents, he hated swearing, violence, and boorish behaviour. Any display of emotion made him uncomfortable. Perhaps it was only natural that he was drawn to music that was cerebral rather than passionate. As Glenn entered his late teens, even his friends noticed that he talked about music as if it were otherworldly.

Glenn was working out his attitudes towards various styles of music and to the whole business of music making, and he didn't hesitate to speak his mind. Playing the piano wasn't enough for him, because he believed himself to be more than just a pianist. "Performing before an audience gave me a glorious sense of power at fifteen," he once said, but even as a teenager, he suspected that giving concerts alone would not satisfy his many creative urges. He already saw himself as being both an artist and an intellectual. He decided that his goal was to be a composer; the piano would provide him with the means.

Ever since Glenn was a child, Florence had encouraged him to compose. To please her, he made up little tunes for which she always praised him. At the conservatory, he excelled at writing fuguettas and devoted hours to analyzing Bach's fugues. Now, he soaked up the techniques of Schoenberg as greedily as he had learned the rules of counterpoint. He came to think of himself as a "valiant defender" of modern music. In his high school essay "My Pet Antipathy," which confounded his teacher, Glenn hints at his growing interest in twentieth-century music and suggests that contemporary composers like Sergei Prokofiev, Francis Poulenc, and Paul Hindemith try to "recapture the pure subjectivity of the Renaissance, Baroque, and Classical eras." No wonder his teacher was dumbfounded. This was heady, sophisticated thinking.

Glenn believed that some modern music was like the great fugues written by Bach: it didn't depend on the fiery flourishes of Romanticism with its cascades of notes, huge robust chords, and heavy reliance on the sustain pedal. While others might think contemporary compositions are passionless and cold, Glenn was attracted to them because to him they represented the rational and the abstract. If he had used colours to describe music, he might have said that the Romantics were hot colours like red, orange, and yellow, whereas the moderns were cool colours like white, blue, and battleship grey.

But he didn't just talk about modern music; he applied what he had learned and composed several pieces including his *Sonata for Piano*. In 1950, he composed the *Sonata for Bassoon and Piano*, which he premiered at the Royal Conservatory with Nicholas Kilburn, a young bassoonist who had given up the piano after he heard Glenn. The room was packed with Toronto's musical intelligentsia. Kilburn was staggered by the turnout. Glenn took it in stride.

They began to play and Kilburn's clip-on bow tie unclipped every time he took a deep breath, so he tossed it on the stand. A moment later, he removed the bassoon's crook and shook it hard to drain the water, but the reed flew off like a dart and landed by the pipes of the organ at the back of the stage. Kilburn didn't have a spare reed. He rose from his chair and muttered, "Vamp 'til ready," as he slipped past Glenn, who was completely oblivious to what had just happened. Kilburn felt like a clown, but he hunted down the reed, cleaned it, and slid it back on the crook. The two finished the piece together.

Soon after he discovered contemporary music, Glenn added it to his repertoire. On October 9, 1949, he gave a recital at the Art Gallery of Ontario in Toronto and included the Sonata no. 7 in B-flat Major, op. 83, by Sergei Prokofiev. Shortly after, he learned Hindemith's Sonata no. 3 in B-flat Major and performed it for the first time on January 19, 1950. Then, he added Alban Berg, and later a concerto by Schoenberg.

That same year Glenn experienced a turning point when he was invited to play on CBC Radio. If Glenn had a constant companion besides his piano and his dog, it was the Canadian Broadcasting Corporation. Founded in 1936, the CBC bound together Canadians separated by vast, empty spaces. Every evening, families huddled around tube radios with polished wooden consoles and fiddled with the plastic controls until the crackling static faded and the announcer's mellifluous voice came through clearly.

Now, Canadians in places like Moose Jaw would hear the young Glenn Gould. On Sunday, December 24, 1950, he arrived at the studio bundled in warm clothes against the harsh winter cold. He took off his coat and eased himself onto the piano bench. In front of him stood a single microphone. On cue, he began to play. The broadcast was live.

Glenn fell in love that morning for the first time in his life. The object of his affection was the studio microphone. Unlike many musicians, he didn't experience the usual jitters in front of a microphone. Several years earlier, he had begun attaching small microphones to his piano to record his practice sessions, and he was one of the first people in Toronto to own a reel-to-reel tape recorder. Until that day in December, however, he had never been inside a real studio. He once described the recording studio as "womb-like" in its security, a place where "time turns in upon itself." No one coughed, sneezed or shuffled. No prying eyes bored into him from a darkened concert hall. He was free to concentrate solely on music making. The studio gave him complete control of the creative process and the microphone put in him in intimate contact with his listeners.

After the performance, the producers presented him with a soft acetate disk of the broadcast. As he looked at it reverently, he caught a "vague impression of the direction" his life would take.

5

On His Own Snowshoes

Slumped in a chair in the conservatory cafeteria, legs crossed and arms folded across his chest, Glenn studied his shoes while several students waited for him to speak. Finally, he said in a deadpan voice, "Mozart really was a bad composer."

"Here we go again," someone scoffed as a few others snorted. Glenn's friends were accustomed to his pronouncements, for they had heard so many over the past few years. "Chopin didn't know how to write anything but short pieces," or "Mozart couldn't write a piano concerto." Once in full flight, Glenn shot off zinger after zinger. Schubert? Well he was "too repetitive." Rachmaninov was "absolutely intolerable." Glenn had no use for ballet and let everyone know it. As for opera, well, it was "rather less than music." Folk music? "I can be charmed by the peasant wrong-headedness of it all." Vladimir Horowitz, the Russian virtuoso who played octaves at warp speed? "He fakes them."

Glenn Gould playing the piano, possibly his Chickering Grand, at the Lake Simcoe cottage, early 1950s. A Bach score sits on top of the piano. Courtesy of the Glenn Gould Estate.

A Musical Force

Glenn's eyes sparkled as he delivered these pithy comments in a charming, humorous way, for he loved to tease people's assumptions. He once shocked a group of teachers by claiming that he could tell them everything about the mechanics of piano playing in a half an hour. Glenn's conservatory acquaintances tolerated his opinions because they sensed he wasn't arrogant. Peter Yazbeck, a fellow piano student, described Glenn as "a sweet guy, really the nicest kid you'd ever want to meet — a gentlemanly kind of kid — but you just talked mainly about musical things with him, and he had his strong opinions at a young age." Robert Fulford said of his teenaged buddy that Glenn had "the most breathtaking confidence I've ever known."

Glenn's peers were aware not only of his views on all matters musical, but also of his remarkable successes. Many attended his recitals and most read the reviews of his performances at the Art Gallery of Toronto (now the Art Gallery of Ontario), Eaton Auditorium, and Hart House. During his late teens, Glenn travelled to Winnipeg, Montreal, Ottawa, as well as several other cities. In the 1950-51 season, he gave recitals in Vancouver and Calgary. Florence accompanied him on his trip west, but never toured with him again. Glenn's friend Ray Dudley said that she was upset because her son was too old for her to control now.

By September of 1952, Glenn had played with the Toronto Symphony Orchestra five times. He was already an exciting, if eccentric, musician. Audiences sat captivated as they watched him crouch low over the keyboard and weave and circle his body while his feet tapped in time with the music. Sometimes, he conducted himself with one hand, index finger jabbing the air, while the other raced along the keys. Not infrequently he sang off-key in a raspy voice that also emitted grunts, moans, yah ta ta ta tas and yah puh puh pums, his lower jaw pumping up and down as energetically as his grandmother's foot had pumped the pedals of her reed organ many years earlier.

Family, friends, Guerrero, and many others implored him to tone down his flagrant displays. The Governor General of Canada himself, Vincent Massey, approached opera singer Maureen Forrester after a recital. "You must tell him to stop it," Massey pleaded. Glenn tried for a few weeks, but couldn't, and in true Gouldian fashion, pronounced that people would have to accept him the way he was.

Between 1947 and 1953, Glenn discovered that the pressure to perform brilliantly intensifies with each concert. He drove himself relentlessly because, deny it as he might, he was ambitious. Yet, the competitive nature of the music world already dismayed him. He had subjected himself to the Kiwanis Music Festival only three times and refused to enter any competition ever again. He eventually grew to dislike playing concertos because they were like a battle between the orchestra and the pianist. He compared the concert hall to the Roman Coliseum and the musicians to gladiators joined in mortal combat. "There is a very curious and almost sadistic bloodlust that overcomes the concert listener," he once said. "I can honestly say that I do not recall ever feeling better about the quality of a performance because of the presence of an audience." Another time he blurted defiantly, "I detest audiences."

Stage anxiety also began to haunt Glenn, although not as severely as it would later. He could already foresee a day when he might quit giving concerts. Years later he told people that he had always known that he would retire from the concert stage at a young age. Perhaps this was a bit of an exaggeration, but even as a teenager, he sensed that the demands of a performing career would always be stressful, and the idea of playing poorly troubled him, even though he had experienced only two minor setbacks as a performer to date.

At the age of eleven, he had played the organ for the choir at St. Simon's Anglican Church in Toronto and for some inexplicable reason kept missing his entrances. He was fired. Another time, his memory failed briefly during a conservatory recital. Glenn panicked. Afterwards, Guerrero taught him to memorize music away from the keyboard. Soon, Glenn astounded people with his ability to study a score and play it from memory and often claimed that he spent more time reading scores in preparation for a concert than actually practising them at the piano.

As he approached twenty, Glenn obsessed more and more about his overall health. Florence still constantly harped about his germs and his posture. "Glenn, please wash your hands. Please sit up straight. Don't eat this, eat that. Don't catch a cold." His back also ached sometimes. Ever since he had fallen off the rail at the cottage years earlier, he had had recurring back pain. Even now his back muscles twinged. Would they act up during a performance? Just the thought that they might, depressed him.

He was also increasingly torn between music and school. Some boys turn to sports or other activities for satisfaction, or they chum around with close friends, join clubs, and go out on dates. Glenn turned inward to his music as a way of dealing with what he described as the "harrowing business of being a teenager." By Grade 13, he had dropped all but two courses: Geography and English. When he applied himself at school, he did well. But for someone so smart, he didn't truly excel, and he blithely ignored his teachers' exhortations to work harder. In hindsight, he said, "I must have been a rather difficult student to handle."

Glenn got along well with his classmates at Malvern, but even as a senior, he avoided the social scene. At home, he directed and acted in short plays. Glenn usually bossed his parents and Jessie into accepting secondary roles while saving the lead for himself. Whenever he felt like company, he either invited a few friends over to his special room or asked Florence to chauffeur him to a party, although the older he grew, the fewer parties he attended. Glenn's presence could dampen everyone's spirits because he detested smoking and couldn't abide swearing, flirting, or drinking. He adamantly refused to dance and his conversations were usually monologues, which, though interesting and often funny, didn't invite any response. Girls found him funny, smart and talented, but he showed no interest in dating. When a reporter asked Florence if her nineteen-year-old son had a girlfriend, "No," she replied primly, "he hasn't time for them yet, and I'm glad he hasn't right now."

All the while, though, unrest was brewing. He was a precocious teenager living with his parents in the Beach, of which Robert once wrote, "For an adolescent, it was a closed, deadening WASP world, a suspicious and narrow and cliquish little compartment in which we all worked hard to avoid knowing both ourselves and our neighbours." Glenn didn't seem to mind the Beach as much as his outspoken friend did, and probably felt quite comfortable there, for although he soared to great heights of artistic daring internally, he also liked his life to be predictable. Yet, he longed for complete independence from his parents, who by now irritated him frequently even though he loved them dearly, especially his mother. He had outgrown them intellectually and musically quite some time ago, but of course he would never tell them that.

Glenn decided to leave Malvern even though he was very close to matriculating. Robert had already quit, claiming that he was "a creative individual in rebellion against a repressive environment."

A Musical Force

Now it was Glenn's turn, and despite the protestations of his parents and even Guerrero, he simply drifted away from school. Shortly after, Glenn shocked his parents again.

"Oh Glenn, surely you aren't serious," Florence said, her voice soft but exasperated. She glanced over at Bert, who sat beside her on the sofa, then back at her son as he paced the living-room floor, his loping gait covering its entire length in just a few steps. Glenn ran his fingers through his sandy hair and waited a few seconds in case Bert had something to add. Bert looked stern but remained silent.

"Actually, mother, I..." Glenn began, but before he could say anything more, Bert suddenly raised his hand like a schoolteacher silencing a chatty pupil. "Glenn. Just listen," he said gruffly. "You want to be a concert pianist, but now you tell us that you intend to quit taking lessons with Alberto Guerrero. That doesn't make any sense."

Glenn opened his mouth to interrupt Bert, but no words came out. He clenched his jaw, shoved both hands into his pockets so his parents wouldn't see them shake, and walked to the bay window. He stared out at the grey sky smudged with clouds. A moment later, he spun around and faced his parents, who now sat mute.

Florence smoothed her skirt, her dark eyes searching Glenn's anxious face. She had much more to say, but for once she bit her tongue. The past year or two, it seemed to her as if her son had nothing good to say about lessons with Guerrero. The three of them remained silent for a few seconds, and then Glenn excused himself and left the room, afraid he might blurt something cruel.

Jessie Greig was sipping tea in the kitchen when Glenn stomped in looking dejected and angry. "Glenn. What's wrong?" she asked, noticing the tears forming in his eyes.

"They just don't understand," he said in a choked voice.

She didn't have to ask another question. Jessie knew that Glenn was tired of piano lessons with Guerrero because he had confided in her many times. Teacher and student disagreed more often than not about repertoire and piano style. Guerrero had also been nagging Glenn about his stage antics.

Jessie also understood Bert and Florence's concerns. Their son was still young and relatively inexperienced. Although he was a local celebrity, Toronto was a long way from the music capitals of Europe and the United States, where he was an unknown. If Glenn wanted a career as a concert pianist, he needed more training and much more exposure because so many other talented young pianists like Van Cliburn and Gary Graffman were vying for the world stage. And then there were the established virtuosos like Arthur Rubinstein and Vladimir Horowitz, who had titillated audiences for years with their pyrotechnical displays. To enter this rarified atmosphere, a young pianist needed not only huge talent, but also expert training, astute management, and extraordinary luck. No one could make it alone. Jessie also knew just how stubborn Glenn could be. She took another sip of tea and said, "I'm sure it will be all right, Glenn," as he marched off to his room.

Glenn slammed the door behind him, dropped into the chair by the radio, and snatched a piece of music from the floor. He slid onto the piano bench a moment later and flipped through the score. When he came to the passage he wanted, he positioned the fingers of his right hand over the correct notes, and with his left index finger, he tapped each finger quickly and precisely with just enough force to make the hammer strike. The sound was even and clean for each note. He moved on to a harder passage and repeated the movement several times. Then he placed the fingers of his left hand over a series of bass notes and tapped them with his right index finger. As each note rang out, he listened intently for the slightest variation in volume and evenness of tone.

Two hours later, drained but satisfied, he sprawled in an easy chair and closed his eyes. Something had to give. He loved living at home, but he needed to be on his own, too. He was almost twenty, and he had big dreams.

That year, 1953, Glenn quit lessons with Guerrero. Florence and Bert were upset and worried. Guerrero didn't believe Glenn was ready to go off on his own even though he had already admitted that he couldn't show Glenn anything more. Guerrero resigned himself to Glenn's decision and wished his pupil well. Gifted teachers and gifted students know that at some point the relationship has to end. The question remained: Is this the right time?

For Glenn it was. His confidence in his decision bordered on arrogance. "Our outlooks on music were diametrically opposed," he told anyone who questioned him about Guerrero. "He was a 'heart' man and I wanted to be a 'head' kid. Besides, nine years is long enough for anyone to be a student of the same teacher. I decided it was time for me to set out on my own snowshoes."

Glenn also claimed that he had taught himself everything he knew about music. This arrogant comment must have hurt Guerrero deeply, but he was a gracious man and said to his wife, Myrtle, "If Glenn feels he hasn't learned anything from me as a teacher, it's the greatest compliment anyone could give me." Guerrero, of course, had guided and nurtured Glenn's prodigious talent in his own unique and self-effacing way.

Glenn's independent spirit had asserted itself once again, and he now set out for the cottage on his metaphorical snowshoes in search of that solitude he craved the way others yearn for social contact. Between 1952 and 1955, he spent much of his time in the bucolic tranquility of the countryside and lived exactly the way he wanted.

6

Becoming Glenn Gould

"Keep lemon in refrigerator — you can take a dessert spoon to make a cup of hot lemonade should you get a cold." Glenn smiled at the spelling mistake in his mother's note. Every time she came to the cottage, Florence left helpful hints taped to the fridge, even though he had been here on his own since he had moved to the cottage two years earlier in 1953. He suspected that she still worried about his decision. But so what if other pianists studied with famous teachers or entered international competitions to gain fame. He was relieved that he didn't have to compete. Compared with most pianists intent on a career, he was an anomaly because his approach was so unorthodox. But he didn't care because he craved this time in semi-seclusion for one important reason, and it wasn't simply to become a great pianist. "My son is becoming Glenn Gould," Bert said.

A relaxed Glenn Gould, November 15, 1958. Courtesy of the Glenn Gould Estate.

A Musical Force

The sun was sinking quickly, and Glenn was famished, for as usual, he had snacked only on Arrowroot cookies and sipped tepid tea all day long. He grabbed his overcoat and cap, stepped over microphone wires strewn like spaghetti across the floor and sidestepped several stacks of scores and books.

He got in his car, turned on CBC Radio full blast and began to conduct the music as he barrelled down the highway twenty miles over the speed limit. As the car straddled the centre line and gobbled up the miles, Glenn leaned over to open the score lying on the passenger's seat — the "suicide seat" as one friend had dubbed it. Years ago, Bert had taught Glenn to drive while holding him on his knee. As a portent of things to come, Glenn had piloted the family car into the lake.

Bill Seto, owner of the Shangri-La Gardens, a restaurant in Orillia, Ontario, stood by the cash register and listened to diners talk and laugh. He glanced out the window and saw a big black car skid to a stop. While the car still shuddered from the sudden jolt, the driver's door opened and a pair of long legs reached for the ground. Seto smiled, and a minute later, a gangly figure dressed in a grey overcoat and matching cap sauntered inside and headed straight to the back booth as several diners gawked at the apparition in heavy wool. This was July and hot. Glenn ignored their staring eyes, sat down, pulled a copy of the *Toronto Daily Star* from his pocket, spread it on the table, and said, "I'll have the usual." The usual was meat and potatoes, Glenn's only real meal of the day.

Around 10:00 p.m., sated and ready to go, Glenn thanked Seto and left, the ritual complete until the next day. He wheeled out of the parking lot and stomped on the accelerator. His new piano waited for him, and he was eager to spend the rest of the night at its ivory keyboard. This instrument was an old turn-of-the-century Chickering baby grand. "It's an extremely solicitous piano with a tactile immediacy almost like a harpsichord's," he muttered to himself as he pulled into the driveway.

Glenn entered the cottage and walked toward the Chickering but was sidetracked by a book that lay open on the table, Thomas Mann's *Dr. Faustus*. He picked up the complex novel and stroked its cover while he contemplated the volumes stacked by the piano. Names of authors like Eliot, Kafka, Schoepenheur, Tolstoy, Dostoevsky, and Plato graced the spines.

Blessed with phenomenal recall, Glenn retained everything he read. Visitors sat spellbound as long convoluted sentences and fat paragraphs loaded with multi-syllabic words flowed easily from his lips. If interrupted, he returned exactly to where he had been a few minutes or an hour earlier. Russian and German authors appealed to him greatly, and when he talked about anything German, he affected a thick accent. Robert said that after Glenn had read *Thus Spake Zarathustra*, his accent became even thicker, which sometimes made him almost unintelligible as he dissected complex ideas and grand themes about life, death, history, music, and art.

What is art? What does it mean to call oneself an artist? How should one live if one wants to be a successful artist? Such questions preoccupied him, and here at Uptergrove, he was forming his own answers. Art was intellectual and it appealed to reason and not to emotion. To create anything of artistic merit, artists had to devote themselves entirely to their passion, and only long periods of solitude allowed this. Everything and everyone else had to be put aside, including family and friends. "You must give up everything else," Glenn told his friend Carl Little.

He dropped Mann's book on the table and practised until dawn.

A Musical Force

Glenn left his sanctuary only to perform or to get away when Florence and Bert arrived. He sometimes chatted with his neighbours and occasionally visited their homes, and he continued to give concerts arranged for him by Homburger.

Shortly after leaving school, he and Robert had concluded that Toronto's dull musical life needed an infusion of the avant-garde. The two ambitious friends formed New Music Associates and produced three concerts between 1952 and 1954. This was a daring, gutsy action in the Toronto of the early 1950s because the city's audiences in those days were skittish about anything new.

Many people thought that Canada was a cultural backwater. While there were plenty of talented musicians, writers, dancers, and artists around, few Canadians knew about them. Still, Glenn was lucky to have been born at the right time. Now in his early twenties, he saw the cultural environment changing. The years after the Second World War were becoming kinder to Canadian artists and musicians. Many cultural institutions were founded in the 1950s. This period saw the birth of the Canada Council, the Canadian Music Council, the Canadian Music Centre, and the Canadian League of Composers. The National Ballet was formed in 1951. The CBC Symphony Orchestra, the Royal Conservatory Opera School, and the CBC Opera Company soon followed.

New Music Associates' first concert featured Schoenberg, and Glenn seized this opportunity to be both performer and educator. He penned the explanatory notes, which were read by a CBC announcer whom they had hired for the occasion. Robert described Glenn's notes as written in the "opaque style later familiar to readers of his liner notes." The announcer confessed he hadn't understood a single word.

For the third and last production, Glenn chose to play Bach, which was ironic because Bach had been dead for centuries. Robert questioned him about his choice. "Bach is ever new," Glenn said and that was that. Of course, things were never that simple with Glenn. He had been practising Bach's *Goldberg Variations* for some time, finger-tapping every one of its thousands of notes, and this was his chance to perform them in public. He had also analysed harpsichordist Wanda Landowska's and pianist Roslyn Tureck's recordings of this magnificent but little-known music. It was to remain so for a while, for the night of the concert, Hurricane Hazel struck Toronto. Traffic stopped, drains filled, and trees toppled. The torrential rain rendered windshield wipers useless. Most people were afraid to leave their homes and only fifteen or so stalwart souls braved the weather that evening. Glenn was disappointed but undaunted because there was so much else to do.

As Glenn's prowess at the keyboard grew, so, too, did his reputation for stubbornness. One day, the Canadian composer Oskar Morawetz visited Glenn at the cottage and brought his new composition *Fantasy in D* for him to play. When Morawetz returned two weeks later, Glenn had already mastered and memorized this complex piece of new music. He played it for Oskar, who remarked on the liberties Glenn was taking with the tempo and pedal markings. Glenn ignored him and performed the piece in public at a much faster pace than Oskar had intended. Finally, when Glenn was about to record the piece, he said to the composer, "Oskar, I won't play it for you at all. I made up my mind how the piece should go, and that's it. When you tell me that one voice is more important than the other one, that's quite incorrect. All voices are equally important. And something else, it seems to me that the way you speak, you don't understand your own music." Oskar listened to the recording once and never again.

In 1954, Glenn was scheduled to play Beethoven's Trio in D Major, *Ghost*, op. 70, no. 1 at the Stratford Music Festival with two outstanding musicians, violinist Alexander Schneider and cellist Zara Nelsova. Glenn showed up for rehearsal with his bottles of water and his already famous chair. As usual he wore an overcoat, muffler, gloves, and hat even though it was a sweltering day.

He adjusted the chair, dropped the score on the piano, and proceeded to play from memory. Schneider and Nelsova pleaded with Glenn to use the music.

"I play by heart," he said, a surprising comment because he sneered at virtuosos who played from memory.

Glenn also debated with the two musicians over interpretation. He had decided how the piece should be played, and he disparaged their polite suggestions.

"How many times have you played this piece?" Schneider asked.

"This is the first time, "Glenn said.

"I've played it four or five hundred times," Schneider countered.

"My position has always been that quality is more important than quantity," Glenn said.

When the three of them finally performed, Glenn sat on his music.

༄

Life at the cottage also gave Glenn an opportunity to explore his other love: composing. He liked to say that by his mid-teens he had made up his mind that he would be a composer. One of his early press kits states, "Mr. Gould hopes to be able to divide his time always equally between composition and the piano." Now that nothing else interfered with his day, Glenn also threw himself into writing music. Even though he refused to admit it, he was at a disadvantage because he lacked training in composition. He had studied theory and counterpoint, but this is not the same as studying composition.

Glenn refused to seek help. Consequently, his first major work, String Quartet in F Minor, op. 1, went slowly. Some days he scratched out only one or two bars. Still, he struggled on alone and completed the work in 1953. The piece was performed on CBC Montreal to a mixed reception. One reviewer said it was "a moving and impressive work," while another wrote that it was "the work of a good student."

Glenn seemed determined to do everything on his own. After hearing him play Bach in Toronto, Harvey Olnick, an American musician, wrote that if Glenn could play other composers as well as he played Bach, "the public will soon be confronted with an artist in no way inferior to Landowska or Serkin." These two were among the elite of musicians. This was gracious praise, but it also implied a "dangerous challenge" according to Glenn's friend Peter Ostwald. Whether Glenn would rise to it or not, remained to be seen. He was still only in his early twenties and had plenty of time to impress his critics with his interpretations of other composers.

Glenn, of course, was studying other composers besides Bach. Recently, he had been working on Beethoven's Sonata no. 30 in E Major, op. 109, which contains an exceptionally tricky passage that Glenn found particularly treacherous. Every time he came to it he choked. He refused to ask anyone for help because

A Musical Force

he was superstitious about his piano technique. "I don't want to think too much about my playing, or I'll get like that centipede who was asked which foot he moved first and became paralyzed just thinking about it," he told journalist Jock Carroll.

Three days before he was to perform the sonata, Glenn still couldn't play the passage without stumbling. In desperation, he fell back on the "last resort method" and turned on two radios full blast to drown out the piano while he practised the passage until he got it. Maybe if he had not been too proud to ask someone, he would have spared himself many hours of anguish, but that wasn't Glenn's way. He had to solve problems with music on his own. Peter Ostwald, who knew Glenn well, said that by this time, "He was listening more to business advisors — his manager, his stockbroker and his accountant." Glenn enjoyed making money, but not because he was greedy. He liked the game of it and relished the challenge of beating the stock market.

Glenn spent more than two happy, contented years at the cottage. This prolonged idyll, however, was now at an end, for Glenn was astute about his career and sensed that he would have to leave Canada to impress people elsewhere. He knew that if artists and musicians wanted to be successful, they had to go to the United States. Glenn loved Canada and never considered leaving permanently, but he also wanted to establish himself internationally.

Program for Town Hall recital, New York, January 11, 1955. This was Glenn Gould's New York debut. Courtesy of the Glenn Gould Estate.

7

A Famous Concert Pianist

On the evening of January 11, 1955, a small audience of thirty-five sat in New York's Town Hall, an inviting place favoured for debuts. Among the attendees were exceptional musicians like Gary Graffman, William Kappell, and Paul Badura-Skoda. Florence, Bert, and Homburger sat in the front row and looked at one another nervously. This was the big time. David Oppenheim, a recording executive with Columbia Records was also there. Before Glenn's New York recital and without telling him, Alexander Schneider, with whom Glenn had played and argued at Stratford, told Oppenheim that Glenn was "alas a little crazy, but had a remarkable, hypnotic effect at the piano." A professional clarinetist himself, Oppenheim had recorded some of the finest performers in the world. A musician would have to be exceptionally good to make him take notice.

Backstage, Glenn was soaking his hands and arms. He had suffered an attack of "fibrositis" earlier, and had spent several hours rushing around New York in search of a "friendly chemist." Glenn had begun to rely on a variety of pain killers and tranquillizers for his many aches, pains, and anxieties, some real and others perhaps imagined. He was understandably excited and very tense. All he had to do was electrify jaded New York critics and brilliant peers.

A few days earlier, on January 2, Glenn had caused quite a buzz with his first American debut recital at the beautiful Phillips Gallery in Washington, D.C. Critic Paul Hume wrote that, "It is unlikely that the year 1955 will bring us a finer piano recital than that played yesterday afternoon in the Phillips Gallery. We shall be lucky if it brings us others of equal beauty and significance." A few musicians telegraphed word of this young new pianist to friends in New York or "Debut Town" as Glenn called it, and now they waited for the young wizard to come onstage.

Glenn appeared a few minutes later, one hand tucked in his pocket. He left the piano's top closed at first, and began to play the same program he had given in Washington: Gibbons's "Earl of Salisbury" Pavane and Galliard, Sweelinck's "Fitzwilliam" Fantasia, five three-part Sinfonias and the Partita in G Major by Bach; Webern's *Variations;* Beethoven's Sonata no. 30 in E Major, op. 109, the one with the "horrible passage" that had given him so much trouble earlier; and Berg's Sonata, op. 1. These were unusual choices for a debut, but Glenn wanted to remain true to himself. "I went out of my way to pick as odd a program as I could," he confessed.

His instincts were good, for from the opening tones of the Gibbons to the closing phrase of the Berg, he held the audience entranced with his musicianship. Applause erupted along with

A Musical Force

cries for an encore at the end of the last piece. People flocked back stage afterwards to congratulate him. The dressing room was abuzz with excitement. "I was absolutely floored by the performance," concert pianist Gray Graffman exclaimed. "It was more than just hearing a very talented newcomer. It was a unique personality already."

"Glenn's playing set such a religious atmosphere that it was just mesmerizing," David Oppenheim echoed.

"Glenn gave them a good concert," Bert told a *Toronto Daily Star* critic, who reported that the concert was a "sensation."

"This was one of the few occasions when I thoroughly loved playing" Glenn said disarmingly as he left to attend a party in his honour.

The moment he stepped into the crowded living room, he regretted coming. People, many of them top musicians, were drinking, smoking, and gossiping. Glenn leaned self-consciously against a wall as several came up to congratulate him. He flinched several times as strangers tried to pat him on the back or squeeze his arm. Sweat beaded on his forehead and his stomach cramped. After a half hour or so, he made a feeble excuse and left abruptly. The hostess, Rosalie Leventritt, turned to Harvey Olnick and said, "What kind of crazy kook have you sent me?"

*

The next morning David Oppenheim offered Glenn an exclusive recording contract based on his debut recital alone. This gesture was unprecedented. Homburger negotiated the terms, but wisely left the choice of music to Glenn, who knew exactly what he wished to record. Other pianists might have selected Beethoven, Mozart, or Chopin for their first major record, difficult music but familiar to the record-buying public, but Glenn turned to his beloved Johann Sebastian Bach and chose the *Goldberg Variations*.

"Don't you think the Two-Part Inventions would be a better debut choice?" one executive asked.

"I'd rather record the *Goldberg Variations*," Glenn said.

"You really would, eh? Well, why not? Let's take a chance," the man replied.

Bach had composed the music for an insomniac, Count Hermann Karl von Keyserling, the former Russian ambassador to Saxony. One of Bach's students played the harpsichord for the Count in hopes the sound would put the man to sleep at night. On a visit to Leipzig, where Bach lived, Keyserling commissioned the composer to write music that might cheer him up during those long sleepless nights. Bach obliged. He had written the *Aria*, the poignant song that introduces the thirty variations, some fifteen years earlier. Now, Bach used the bass line to this plaintive melody as the foundation upon which he constructed one of the most intricate and inventive pieces of keyboard literature.

Few people at the time played this music; fewer still knew of its existence. Wanda Landowska and Roslyn Tureck, both highly regarded musicians, had more or less made the *Goldberg Variations* their own. Glenn, himself, had performed them on CBC Radio, at the Stratford Festival, and a few intimate recitals. Harvey Olnick heard Glenn's version of Bach's masterpiece several years earlier at the University of Toronto and was absolutely "thunderstruck." "Where did you learn to play Bach like this?" he had asked Glenn.

Where indeed? Glenn could be so secretive. Florence had introduced him to *The Well-Tempered Clavier*; Guerrero opened many more of Bach's mysteries. As for the *Goldberg Variations*, Glenn said, "This was a work which I learned entirely on my own.

A Musical Force

I never really had a lesson with anyone on it and in fact it was one of the works that I did learn entirely without my teacher." Glenn had spent hours analyzing Bach's delightfully inventive contrapuntal lines and finger-tapping every one of its thousands of notes. He marvelled at the way Bach wove so many voices together and brought them all to a satisfying ending in each variation, only to create new permutations in subsequent ones.

Glenn once said that Bach "led an extraordinary journey." Now, five years into the 1950s, Glenn was undertaking his own extraordinary journey, and the first stop was an old church on East 30th Street in New York, where Columbia had a recording studio, and where every day throughout one week in June, 1955 Glenn hunkered over a Steinway grand while the tapes rolled. The studio technicians enjoyed the spectacle of watching Glenn stride in dressed in overcoat, muffler, beret, and gloves, and carrying bags bulging with bottles of Poland Water, boxes of biscuits and cookies, towels, and assorted pills. The folding chair Bert had lovingly altered a couple of years earlier so Glenn could sit exactly 14 inches off the floor was ever-present. The air-conditioning engineer was on constant alert in case Glenn complained about temperature changes. Glenn religiously tested the piano every day before signalling he was ready to work. If he grew hungry, Arrowroot biscuits washed down with water or skim milk hit the spot. Here, in a bare, spacious room, Glenn was alone with a piano, microphone, and J.S. Bach. It was paradise.

Day after day, hour after hour, take after take, Glenn focused completely on the music.

"That's really good, Glenn," the producer would say.

"We'll see," Glenn would reply and immediately start over again.

He taped each variation many times and listened to every playback as he wandered around studio, eyes half-closed, shirt open, and baggie pants low on his waist. Enthralled by the sound, he sometimes swayed to the music as arms gracefully swept the air while his gangly body turned around and around. Columbia released the recording in 1956. Glenn's vision of the music was profoundly different from that of Roslyn Tureck or Wanda Landowska, and it instantly appealed to thousands of people. A huge commercial success, Glenn's first major recording has never been out of print since.

The record jacket features thirty-two black and white photos of Glenn. Here is Glenn playing Bach's music as if he were creating it. He pours all his youthful passion and soul into the music, but never at the expense of that quick analytical mind of his. Glenn's *Goldberg Variations* pulse with restless rhythmic energy. The touch is sure, every voice given equal importance. The devilishly difficult ornaments are gracefully etched and the long breathless phrases are perfectly sculpted. The sound is vibrant, at times ringing and stately, at times delicate and melancholy, and at times cheerful and frolicking. No one had ever heard Bach played this way.

In the liner notes, Glenn, a young man possessed of an uncanny ability to analyse complex musical structures and bring out their inner beauty, wrote the following words for his recording of Bach's creation: "It is, in short, music which observes neither end nor beginning, music with neither real climax nor real resolution, music which, like Baudelaire's lovers, 'rests lightly on the wings of the unchecked wind.'"

Glenn made Bach's magnificent work his own. He had persevered despite the initial doubts some had about such a recording, and now anyone who played this music would be compared to him. World-renowned musicians and conductors like Leonard Bernstein and Herbert von Karajan were stunned by this recording, for this was musicianship of the highest order: daring, innovative, and exuberant. In a word — new. Aaron Copeland, the great American composer, said that "the unnerving thing about Glenn playing Bach was that it was as if Bach himself was performing."

Suddenly, this young oddball pianist from Canada was a celebrity. *Life* magazine featured him in a four-page photo essay. He was in *Glamour* and *Vogue* magazines. This kind of press was usually reserved for pop musicians and movie stars, and Glenn revelled in the publicity. Writers called him a "hipster." He was "cool." Classical music lovers adored the record. Jazz musicians tapped their feet to his rhythmic playing. Glenn was gratified by the attention, and proud that he had made people take notice without sacrificing his artistic integrity. When he was a toddler, he had said that he would be a famous concert pianist. Now he was.

That year, 1956, Glenn splurged on a new car. It was a Plymouth. Glenn loved big cars, the bigger the better. A car was like the recording studio. Sitting on the plush seat, windows up, and radio on, he was insulated from the outside and in complete control. As he drove the sedan home, he contemplated his future and how bright it looked. Offers for concerts poured in, and a short while after the release of the album, Homburger announced that the 1956–57 concert season was fully booked.

Glenn was happy, but he was tired, too. The past months had been gruelling and unusually stressful with the twin U.S. debuts, concerts in Ottawa, Toronto, and Montreal, and the recording sessions in New York. His sudden popularity had placed incredible strain on him. At one point in New York, he had to go to Emergency, and shortly after finishing the *Goldberg Variations*, he secretly sought out a psychiatrist because he had been quite anxious for a while. He had trouble eating, and his stomach had been terribly upset, more so than usual. He was worried that he might have an eating disorder.

Glenn needed to refresh himself with a break from this crazy pace. Accompanied by journalist Jock Carroll, he flew to the Bahamas. Florence asked Jock to coax her son out into the sun. Good luck. Ever the doting mother, she also asked Jock to make sure that Glenn sent his clothes to the laundry and that he bought some decent clothes. Good luck, again.

At first, Glenn stayed cooped up in the hotel. He avoided the sun, and shied away from saltwater because he thought it might hurt his hands. One afternoon, he took Jock out in a motorboat and raced recklessly around the island, narrowly missing a freighter. Jock was terrified. A few days later, Glenn rented a car and introduced the locals to the Gould style of driving.

One evening Glenn confided in Jock about a recurring dream in which he saw himself being swept over Niagara Falls. At the last second, he managed to grab a rock, but faceless strangers banged his hands to make him lose his grip. At this point, he would wake up. The dream was probably evidence of the great pressure he had endured in the past months. Glenn liked to say, "There's a cloud behind every silver lining." Perhaps he sensed that his future would be trying.

Glenn returned home and played with great verve to a full house at Massey Hall. Probably never in its history had the old building heard such applause. The hoarse calls for encores kept him at the piano for three hours, and he basked in the glory. The next day, the mayor presented him with an engraved wristwatch, and the following day, the *Globe and Mail* featured him on its front page. The shy, gentle man with the charming smile and engaging sense of humour had made the entire country proud of him.

That December Glenn appeared with the Winnipeg Symphony Orchestra. The audience treated him like a pop star and applauded his performance endlessly. Glenn was now on the verge of international fame. The past year had brought many rewards, but it had also taken its toll.

"How do you feel about all your success?" a reporter asked. Glenn, an enigmatic smile on his face, tipped back in the chair and hugged his chest. "Well, it meant a great deal to me," he said as the interviewer hastily scribbled in his notebook. "But it also launched me into the most difficult year I have ever faced." Before the reporter could ask another question, Glenn excused himself and left.

Glenn Gould taking a bow on stage in Russia, May 1957. Courtesy of the Glenn Gould Estate.

8

"That Nut's a Genius"

After the success of his first major record, Glenn went on to his next triumph, Beethoven's Piano Concerto no. 4 in G Major, op. 58 with the Detroit Symphony Orchestra on March 15, 1956. He played brilliantly even though he was still suffering from the eating disorder that had caused him so much trouble earlier. The audience rewarded him with six curtain calls, but a few reporters panned his theatrical mannerisms. The *Detroit Free Press*, in particular, was quite cutting: "Gould's storm-tossed mane of hair, his invertebrate posture at the keyboard and his habit of collapsing at the end of each solo line was sheer show business."

Just before his solo recital in Toronto a few weeks later, Glenn found a new doctor to prescribe him more drugs to add to his growing arsenal of medication. Then he performed at Stratford in the summer of 1956, which pleased him because in this quaint Ontario town he had some control over the artistic direction of the music. For one glorious evening, he astounded the audience as he played and conducted from the piano a concert for which he had also written the program notes. He hinted to a group of admirers that one logical solution to his career "is to retire from the piano and devote myself solely to conducting, which I'm seriously considering doing." After Stratford, he headed back to the United States where he was toasted in Pasadena, Dallas, St. Louis, and San Francisco.

Although his schedule was crammed with concerts, Glenn also made time for recording. After completing the *Goldberg Variations*, he had returned to the studio to record in February of 1956 Bach's Partita no. 5 in G Major, a work he had played many times on tour. He immediately found fault with the studio piano and compensated for its deficiencies by singing louder than ever. Howard Scott, the Columbia recording director, listened to the duel between Glenn's voice and the piano.

"Look, Glenn, we can hardly hear the piano because you're singing so loud," Scott yelled.

"Look, Howard, it's the piano not me," Glenn said, slightly miffed. He glanced up at the booth a beat and added, "Suppose, I wear a gas mask while I play. Then you won't have to hear me sing."

Howard shook his head and suggested they take a break and try another piano later.

A few months after this session, Glenn returned to the studio to begin what would be his second major recording for Columbia, the last three piano sonatas of Ludwig van Beethoven. Glenn admitted that he felt "ambivalent" about the famed composer's work, and had once told an interviewer, "But even in these early years, Mr. Beethoven and I did not see eye to eye on what constitutes good music."

Perhaps, but Glenn did admire Beethoven's late piano sonatas, and he chose them for his second major recording, even though many believed that at twenty-four, he lacked the musical maturity to do them justice. Glenn disagreed. He was experimenting with and exploring music, intent on discovering something no one else had noticed. He went to the studio: take one, take two, take three and so on. Afterwards, the task of editing began according to Glenn's own "splicing plan," which let the engineers know which segments of tape were to be used and which discarded.

Anticipation was high after the phenomenal popularity of the *Goldberg Variations*. Many people unfortunately were disappointed with the new disc and some harsh criticism followed. Harold Schonberg of the *New York Times* wrote, "Not only are the performances immature; they are actually inexplicable." Glenn had ignored several of Beethoven's strict tempo markings, so the public spanking was to be expected. When one interviewer questioned him directly about his interpretation, Glenn turned to the man and said defensively, "If there's any excuse at all for making a record, it's to do it differently. And if one can't quite do that, I would say, abandon it, forget about it, move on to something else."

⚜

In January 1957, Glenn debuted with the renowned New York Philharmonic under the baton of Leonard Bernstein. Glenn wound his way past the orchestra, fitted himself to his chair, wrapped right leg over left during the opening bars of Beethoven's Piano Concerto no. 2 in B-flat Major, and stared at the keyboard, right foot beating the air in time to the music. Then, he untangled his legs and played with great personality. "He is the greatest thing that has happened to music in many years!" Bernstein exclaimed.

A few weeks later during a rehearsal of Beethoven's Piano Concerto no. 3 in C Minor, Bernstein said, "Glenn, let's go to my place for dinner." Glenn agreed and put on his coat, muffler, and gloves. He plopped an astrakhan hat on top of the cap he was already wearing while Bernstein watched in silent amusement. When the two entered the stylish apartment, Bernstein's wife Felicia said, "Oh, aren't you going to take off your hat?"

"Well, I don't think so," Glenn replied, only to comply a few minutes later. Felicia's eyes widened when she saw the sweaty, mattered head of hair that hadn't been washed or trimmed in a very long time. Here before her was the young man whose first recording had comforted her during the last month of her pregnancy.

"But this is impossible," she gasped at the unkempt hair. Leonard excused himself and went to make drinks while Glenn stared sheepishly at the floor. Before he could utter a word, Felicia steered him gently toward the bathroom, sat him on a stool and shampooed his hair until it was golden. Then she gave him a proper haircut.

In March of 1957, Glenn debuted with the Cleveland Orchestra. At the rehearsal, the orchestra waited patiently while he tinkered with his chair, turning its screws to get the right height. Finished, he sat down ready to play, but just as the musicians raised their instruments in anticipation of the downbeat. Glenn knelt down again and began fiddling with the screws. After several more failed attempts, he demanded that a carpenter be hired to build blocks so the piano could be raised. George Szell, the conductor, sniped, "Perhaps if I were to shave a sixteenth of an inch off your derrière, Mr. Gould, we could begin." The papers printed the comment, which Glenn immediately denied. "If Szell had said something so insulting," Glenn protested, "the Cleveland Orchestra would have been looking for a new soloist that evening." Szell, however, admired Glenn's musicianship and later said to his assistant, "That nut's a genius."

Glenn continued to travel around Canada and the United States. During the 1957–58 season, he gave more than thirty concerts and fifty the following season. His antics frequently raised eyebrows. At one recital, he caused a stir when he strolled onstage dressed in an ill-fitting business suit instead of a tuxedo. His suits were usually dark and baggy, and sometimes when he slipped off his shoes, the audience would titter at his mismatched socks.

His clothing may have been sloppy, but his playing electrified audiences. Glenn was an iconoclast who refused to include pieces sure to be crowd pleasers. Glenn always denied that he was a teacher, but he loved to challenge listeners to experience music the way he did. At a few recitals, he lectured almost as much as he played. In Vancouver, an audience member, frustrated with his interminable rambling, rose from her seat and said, "We've paid a lot of money for tickets to your concert, so please shut up and play."

Reviewers picked on his mannerisms, the Poland Water, untied shoes, mismatched socks, oriental carpet, and rickety chair. Harold Schonberg of the *New York Times* wrote, "Why not a ham sandwich and beer?" Yet audiences found him endearing and mysterious. Pianists, students, and curious admirers swarmed around him after every performance. He answered nosy questions about his medications and the insurance on his hands, which were now insured with Lloyd's of London for $100,000. He had come a long way from just a few years earlier when he was afraid to shake hands with well-wishers and instead had handed out a card that read in part: "A pianist's hands are sometimes injured in ways which cannot be predicted. Needless to say, this could be quite serious."

※

Several months earlier, in 1956, Glenn had been invited to perform in Russia, which was a great honour because he would be the first Canadian musician and the first North American pianist to perform in that country. Relations between the U.S.S.R. and the West had been poor since the end of the Second World War, when the two powers entered a period called the Cold War. For many years, mutual mistrust prevented any kind of cultural exchange. By 1957, political leaders in the Soviet Union decided to open the barrier between them and Canada in an effort to encourage trade and cultural activities. Homburger lined up concerts in Moscow and St. Petersburg, which was then called Leningrad. He also arranged concerts in Berlin and Vienna.

If the tour proved successful, Glenn's fame would grow. He was excited, but also apprehensive about Russian food and hotel rooms. In a letter to a fan in Quebec, Glenn wrote, "In two weeks I shall be off for Russia ... if my stomach holds up with the Russian food, I imagine that I shall have a really fascinating time." With Homburger, he was more direct. "I can see the Canadian Press writing from Moscow: '"Gould Throws Up,"' he said as the two prepared to leave.

The trip over was uneventful. Glenn seemed at ease on the airplane, and chatted amiably with Homburger or thumbed a copy of *Say It in Russian*. After they arrived, the two of them headed straight for the hotel. Later, Glenn stayed at the Canadian Embassy in Moscow because he was displeased with his accommodations at the expensive hotel. He and Homburger roamed

A Musical Force

the city's tree-lined streets, marvelled at the alien architecture, and visited several museums before they returned to the embassy to mingle with diplomats and dignitaries, whose small talk, toasts, and interminable speeches bored Glenn to tears. One evening, a very attractive woman, the wife of one of the diplomats, cornered Glenn and tried to seduce him. He was horrified by her brazen advances and didn't know how to respond, so he pretended she wasn't there.

※

On May 7, 1957, Glenn performed Bach, Beethoven, and Berg in the Great Hall of the Moscow State Conservatory. In deference to his hosts' wishes, he wore a tuxedo for the occasion. The hall, which seated 1,800, was less than half full. He played four fugues and the Partita no. 6 all by Bach, and the hall exploded with applause. People streamed out at intermission to call their friends and when Glenn returned onstage for the second half, he faced a packed house. He played with great energy and imbued each piece with his special magic. The Russians, enraptured by his unique pianism and machine-gun technique, sat still. Then, they heard something completely unexpected: the sonata by Berg. The sudden intrusion of a modern composition caught them off guard, because this kind of music was forbidden in the Soviet Union. Modern art, literature, and composition were considered to be products of the decadent West. Few Russians had seen paintings by Picasso or heard music composed by Schoenberg and Webern.

"Bravo! Bravo!" people shouted well before the concert's end. The applause swelled, then slowly turned into a deafening, rhythmic clapping that filled the hall. This was the Russians' highest compliment. Glenn bowed and a giant basket of blue chrysanthemums suddenly appeared onstage while voices shouted for encore after encore. The next evening Glenn played at Tchaikovsky Hall with the Moscow Philharmonic Orchestra. A few nights later, he appeared at this famous venue and endeared himself to the Russians with the *Goldberg Variations*, a piece by Brahms, and Hindemith's Sonata no. 3 in B-flat Major.

Glenn gave a recital and talk at the Moscow Conservatory of Music on May 12. He chose forbidden music: Berg, Schoenberg, Krenek, and Webern. Students and teachers grumbled nervously. What would the authorities say if they found out? A few disgruntled professors walked out in disgust, but everyone else stayed. People pleaded with Glenn to play Bach and Beethoven, but he refused because he was determined to introduce them to contemporary music. He eventually relented and as an encore played some Bach. The iconoclasm of his interpretation, his graceful technique, his relentless energy and rhythmic, almost dance-like playing elicited gasps of admiration from the audience. The ovation was deafening. Glenn, sweat pouring from his forehead, took many bows. *This has to be the most exciting occasion in which I have taken part*, he thought as he beamed at his hosts. Soon after, he travelled to Leningrad, where the hall was packed to overflowing and extra chairs were brought onstage. People again showered the stage with flowers and applauded madly.

Russians loved Glenn and cheered or embraced him in boisterous bear hugs whenever they saw him on the street. Glenn had always been averse to physical demonstrations of any kind, but he good-naturedly tolerated being smothered by his Russian fans.

Glenn thoroughly enjoyed his stay in Russia. He must have felt comfortable, for he even went sightseeing on his own. Ever observant, he wrote a letter to his new dog, Banquo, in which he informed his beloved pet of the state of Russian dogs, stating that there were few dogs here because most were killed in the war. He ended by suggesting, "You would have the field all to yourself if you were here." On their part, the Russians would never forget this stranger who appeared as if from Mars.

The next stop was Berlin, Germany, one of the undisputed music centres of Europe and home of the famous conductor Herbert von Karajan and the Berlin Philharmonic Orchestra. From the opening bars of Beethoven's Piano Concerto no. 3 in C Minor, Karajan's magnetic personality mesmerized Glenn, and he followed every arabesque of the diminutive conductor's graceful baton. The critical German audience burst into applause when the final chord sounded and Glenn lowered his head and thought, *This is one of the truly indelible musical-dramatical experiences of my life.* The concert was a huge success. One journalist compared Glenn with Ferruccio Benvenuto Busoni, who was regarded as a musical and intellectual giant.

After Berlin, Glenn travelled to Vienna, Austria. As the train wound its way past tidy fields and stands of trees, he settled back and relaxed. *This is the most wonderful pastorale imaginable,* he thought before he closed his eyes and drifted off to sleep.

At Frankfurt station, Glenn spied an elderly, white-haired man strolling up and down the platform. It was Leopold Stokowski, who had gained great fame as the conductor of Walt Disney's *Fantasia*, a film Glenn had hated when he first saw it as a young boy in a Toronto theatre because its "riotous colour" made him feel ill. Glenn, desperate to meet the renowned musician, purposefully dropped his train ticket in Stokowski's path, stooped to pick it up, then cocked his head as the conductor approached and with feigned incredulity said, "Why, it's ... it's ... it's Maestro Stokowski, isn't it?"

"It is, young man," Stowkowski replied resignedly.

"I am Glenn Gould."

"I have read that you were recently in Leningrad," Stokowski said.

Glenn was thrilled. The famous man had heard of him. They met later to discuss their respective impressions of that city. Glenn confided in a friend that he would have been pleased to hear Stokowski's impression of Mickey Mouse if it meant a visit with the great conductor, for Glenn greatly admired the elderly man, whom he called an "ecstatic."

In Vienna, Glenn again conjured ethereal tones from the piano and held both audiences and critics spellbound. And then the tour was over. Herbert von Karajan generously offered to introduce Glenn to any city in which he was conducting. The future looked good for a return to Europe, but it was time to go home. Glenn toyed with the idea of renting a car to do some sightseeing, but changed his mind. His hosts never had the pleasure of experiencing his enthusiastic driving. Glenn was homesick. He missed Toronto, where he could read Shakespeare and play badminton with his friends in the Lower Rosedale Shakespeare Reading and Badminton Society, a group that had formed a couple of years earlier. Besides, he felt a cold coming on.

9

"Let's Ban Applause"

One afternoon in late December of 1958, Glenn sat in a rented car and stared at the sand dunes near Tel Aviv, Israel. The previous months had been gruelling. After returning home from his first overseas tour, he had given more than twenty concerts in Canada and the United States. The frantic pace had made him edgy and at times ill mannered. In Buffalo, Glenn had sent a stage attendant out to place an oversized score of Beethoven's third on the piano. Then he instructed the poor man to place a glass of water by the music while he waited nervously in the wings. After several more minutes elapsed, he ambled onstage to whispers and polite applause, seated himself at the piano, and he twisted his torso so his back was to the audience. The conductor raised his baton and Glenn crossed his legs and cupped his chin in his left hand. He remained in this frozen pose throughout the entire opening *tutti* section. A few weeks later in Boston, he had

Glenn Gould was awarded the Harriet Cohen Bach Medal in 1959. Courtesy of the Glenn Gould Estate.

A Musical Force

unceremoniously announced that he would substitute a Mozart sonata for the programmed Beethoven sonata because he hadn't practised enough.

He had grown increasingly agitated as the tour progressed, and the prospect of three months in Europe had begun to seem ridiculous. "Well, who the hell said it was supposed to be fun anyway?" he had blurted before boarding the plane for Salzburg. While there he had contracted a touch of tracheitis, which led to a kidney infection and forced him to spend a month convalescing in Hamburg. Now, he was near the end of a grinding two-week tour of Israel and in just a few hours he was to play Beethoven's Piano Concerto no. 2 in B-flat Major in Jerusalem. The morning rehearsal had been a disaster because the piano was "absolutely rotten." Glenn said he had played "like a pig." Desperate to find a solution, he had driven out the countryside to be alone with his thoughts.

Glenn closed his eyes, settled back in the car seat and let the desert stillness soothe him as his mind wandered to Uptergrove and his beloved Chickering piano. He mentally stroked its worn keys and imagined its light, crisp tone in his mind. He sat like this for an hour, his fingers never moving while in his mind's eye they formed complex chords and tripped delicately through arpeggios and torturous chords and runs. Finished and feeling ready for that evening's concert, he started the car. He fought the urge to stomp on the accelerator, and drove back to the motel a bit more cautiously than he had the other day when he had collided with a truck. "The driver was blind," Glenn had offered as an explanation to concerned Israelis.

That evening he strode onto the freezing stage wearing his overcoat and scarf. Thoughtful attendants had placed a dozen heaters onstage, but they didn't help much. Glenn played superbly despite the miserable conditions. One critic wrote, "Gould touches the piano and there you are captivated by those fantastic hands and you listen to his playing and you feel that it comes from another planet."

Glenn was justifiably proud of his performances in Israel, but he was exhausted and "terribly depressed" because being on the road simply disagreed with him. The foreign food, hotel rooms, and the constant tension that began every morning and built by evening — all took their toll. Rather than rebooking his cancelled performances in Europe, he went home, but not for long. The day after Christmas of 1958, he resumed touring and gave thirty concerts in four months in North America before flying overseas to London, where audiences received him warmly, but critics pummelled him for his stage deportment. He garnered the same praise as he had everywhere else. As before, though, Glenn developed various illnesses, or the "inevitable European flu, the ache-all-over feeling we hear about in the Alka-Seltzer ad," as he described in a letter to his worried parents.

In February 1959, he received a great honour — the Harriet Cohen Bach Medal. In June, he travelled to New York and took a taxi to Columbia's studio. He fiddled with his cap and tugged on his lapels while the cabbie navigated the busy streets, then leaned forward and said, "Sorry, I don't want to roast you out," Glenn said, "but do you think we could have the window up a little bit?"

"Why, don't you feel well?" the cabbie said.

"I'm from Canada. Up there we're used to having the windows up."

"Canada? What kind of place is Canada? Where in Canada?"

"A little place. You've probably never heard of it. Uptergrove."

"Uptergrove. This must be like a place we got somewhere in the backwoods — Oshkosh," the cabbie said pulling up to the curb. "What do you do at Columbia Records?"

"I'm a pianist," Glenn mumbled, pronouncing it "pyahnist."

"A what?" the cabbie asked frowning.

"A musician."

"What do you play? Longhair music? Jazz? Bebop?"

"Oh, I'm the longhair variety."

"You must have a beautiful audience. They must be falling asleep on you."

Glenn grimaced and exited the cab. Inside the studio, he greeted the producer and began a week-long recording session of Bach's *Italian Concerto*. The session was the subject of one of two documentaries filmed by the National Film Board of Canada: *Glenn Gould: Off the Record* and *Glenn Gould: On the Record*. "This movie making has done more for my morale and, indeed, enthusiasm for life in general than anything else within memory," he wrote to a friend in London.

Fall came and Glenn flew to Europe and more drudgery: strange hotel rooms, long train rides, and peculiar food. As if on cue, he caught a cold again and cancelled two concerts in Salzburg, but managed to play the remaining date. Fortunately, he made the concert in Lucerne where he performed Bach's Concerto in D Minor with the Philharmonia. Glenn had stunned von Karajan several months earlier with his pianism at a rehearsal of the same concerto with the Berlin Philharmonic. After just a few bars, Von Karajan cocked his silver-haired head in amazement, laid his baton on the stand, and sat down in the front row to listen while Glenn and the orchestra played on without him.

Now, almost a year later, Glenn sat on the stage at Lucerne surrounded by string players while the German maestro's baton carved the air from the lip of the stage. Glenn again truly touched both the esteemed conductor and the audience with his sensitive, intelligent musicianship. "Did it really take a young Canadian to show us how to play Bach?" one critic wrote. After this concert, Glenn returned home never to visit Europe again.

⁂

Glenn wandered through the palatial twenty-six-room country estate called Donchery. He pulled back the curtains on the window that looked out over the tennis court and swimming pool. This place certainly met his "longing for grandeur" as he told John Roberts, who had been urging him to move out of his parents' home. At twenty-seven, Glenn was more than ready for a place of his own. Several months earlier, he had tried living in the Windsor Arms in Toronto, a lovely hotel John Lennon and Yoko Ono would stay in a few years later. But he had grown tired of hotel rooms and desired a more permanent residence, so he kept shopping around until he found and leased this palatial dwelling outside Toronto. He looked once more at the tennis court and swimming pool he wouldn't use and suddenly felt embarrassed by his extravagance. He would simply have to back out of the lease and keep house hunting.

Early in 1960, he acquired a six-room penthouse apartment on St. Clair Avenue West in Toronto. This apartment became home for the rest of his life even though he rented other places from time to time. Several years later he also rented a studio apartment at the Inn on the Park in Toronto, where he did much of his tape editing.

Alberto Guerrero died the same year Glenn moved out on his own. Glenn hid his feelings and said little, but he must have been saddened by the death of this gentle man who had nurtured his talent. Glenn had never publicly acknowledged his debt to his mentor, but he had privately sought Guerrero's advice on occasion and had also recommended students to his old teacher. Glenn's friend Ray Dudley always said, "Never was there a sign of a split with them." Others disagreed.

Shortly after Guerrero's death, Glenn visited Steinway & Sons in New York. He tested a few of their elegant instruments, then went to the office Winston Fitzgerald, the official in charge of artists and repertory, to discuss pianos. Glenn had such special requirements that not even a Steinway could really meet them, and he often presumptuously advised the firm about how to improve its instruments. He wanted a piano with a tone that sounded "a little like an emasculated harpsichord." He also said he didn't like the piano as an instrument and preferred the harpsichord. His ideal piano was the graceful Chickering he had discovered a few years earlier. Its light, delicate action suited his technique perfectly. Glenn's quest to find the perfect piano truly never ended although he came close when he discovered the Steinway CD 318 model.

Fitzgerald and Glenn were in deep discussion when William Hupfer, the firm's chief concert technician, walked in and gently patted Glenn's shoulder in greeting. Glenn cringed from the touch.

"Glenn, what's wrong?" Fitzgerald asked after Hupfer left.

Glenn, a gloomy look on his face replied, "He hurt me."

A few days later, Glenn complained about pain in the same shoulder. He visited five doctors for treatments. One of them placed Glenn's upper body in a plaster cast for a short while. Glenn cancelled his upcoming concerts. The alleged shoulder injury became a convenient excuse to cancel future concerts. Despite the injury, however, he did make his important American television debut in January 31, 1960, as well other concerts that appealed to him.

Against the advice of friends, Glenn sued Steinway & Sons because he really believed that Hupfer had injured him. He was, after all, physically delicate, and the fall from the rail at the cottage years ago still bothered him. But he was also a hypochondriac whose limitless imagination magnified even the slightest discomfort. The lawsuit was settled out of court, and Steinway paid Glenn just over $9,000. Glenn behaved like a gentleman throughout the embarrassing ordeal. In 1961, Frederick Steinway wrote a memo to his employees requesting that they avoid any physical contact with him. Glenn continued to play Steinways and to give technical advice about how to set them up to his satisfaction.

❧

These years were a mixed blessing for Glenn. He was being paid handsomely, but he was truly torn because the more he performed, the more he disliked it, and as his career progressed, he became ill frequently, which led to inevitable cancellations. After the second European tour, he appeared onstage less often, but still cancelled bookings. He quipped, "I don't go to concerts — not even my own." Witty comments like that one, however, masked a profound and growing dissatisfaction with the whole business of live music making, which he said made him feel like a vaudevillian.

Glenn had confessed many times that he hated competition and that he disagreed with the whole grading system so prevalent in music education, a system which forced students to try to beat each other. You're worth an A while someone else is only a B or

A Musical Force

C, and so on. Where was the joy in music if one had to compete? Most of all, Glenn didn't want to sit on a stage and have people stare at him. When it came to playing concertos with orchestras, he felt even more disgruntled.

Other interests made huge demands on his time. Glenn recorded sixteen albums for CBS between 1955 and 1963 and wrote the liner notes for eight of them. Each trip to the studio convinced him that the future of music lay in recording, which for Glenn was an art form in itself with "its own laws and its own liberties, its quite unique problems and its quite extraordinary possibilities." He foresaw the day when musicians would compose, record, and edit their creations. He believed that with future technology "a new kind of listener" would emerge, one would be an interactive creator and not just passive receptacles of sound "I'm all for the kit concept," he argued. "I'd love to issue a series of variant performances and let the listeners choose what they themselves most like. Let them assemble their own performance." At the time, his ideas sounded far-fetched, yet, today, any person with a computer can sample music.

At the same time, Glenn was also convincing himself, if no one else, that the age of live concerts would soon come to an end even as music was becoming a major social force in North America. During the next decade, the Beatles, the Rolling Stones, Bob Dylan, Joan Baez, Joni Mitchell, Neil Young and dozens of others would draw huge crowds to their concerts.

More than anything, Glenn desired a meaningful exchange between musicians and audiences, a dialogue that in his opinion was impossible to achieve in a traditional concert hall. He hoped to reach and to teach people through recorded music. Glenn embraced technology and agreed with those who argued that someday technology would liberate people. Now, free from the burden of live performance, he threw himself into recording and mercilessly drove everyone involved. Every detail, no matter how minute, received his undivided attention.

Although Glenn argued against the value of concerts, he did enjoy himself at a few of his own. In 1961, at a recital billed as *A Piano Lesson with Glenn Gould* he had a great deal of fun lecturing three thousand young people. The next year, he returned to Stratford for a Bach concert and told audience members that applause was an easily induced mob reaction. He ordered them not to respond, and dimmed the house lights completely for the final fugue to make his point. "Applause tells me nothing," he told one of the bemused reporters. "Like any other artist, I can always pull off a few musical tricks at the end of a performance and the decibel count will automatically go up ten points." The same year he wrote his essay "Let's Ban Applause" in which he states somewhat pompously that "the most efficacious step which could be taken in our culture today would be the gradual but total elimination of audience response."

For the final concert of the Stratford season, he sauntered onstage dressed in black cap, knee-high olive green socks, and baggy beige pants and said, "You didn't expect music did you? My name is Plummer." The audience giggled at this reference to Christopher Plummer, the Canadian actor. Glenn launched into a pedantic lecture about Schoenberg and neo-Classical music, which some couldn't hear and others found dull. When people began to leave, he apologized and said, "I'm tired."

"So are we," a voice answered from the hall.

Glenn's antics and provocative statements annoyed many. Composer Udo Kasments wrote in the *Toronto Daily Star* that he had hoped "the pampered wonder-boy would grow up and concentrate on straight and honest music making. Time has proved me wrong. Glenn Gould has changed indeed, but the change has been for the worse."

Glenn wasn't trying to upset people, nor was he simply fooling around. He found much about the music world unpalatable — the pettiness, the competition, and the unrelenting pressure to play perfectly. Probably his feelings were coloured as well by his anxiety. Like many musicians, he frequently experienced stage fright and increasingly relied on medication to deal with it.

❧

On April 5, 6, and 8 of 1962, Glenn was scheduled to perform the Brahms Piano Concerto no. 1 in D Minor with the New York Philharmonic, conducted by Leonard Bernstein. A few days before the performance, Bernstein picked up his phone and heard Glenn gush, "Oh boy, have I got some surprises for you; I have made such discoveries about this piece."

"Along what order?" Bernstein asked, "You're not making a big cut."

"No, no," Glenn replied. "It's just a matter of tempo here and there, but I just want to warn you because you might be a little choked."

On Thursday, April 5, they performed at the preview concert, during which Bernstein usually gave a short talk about the music. The maestro approached Glenn backstage a few minutes before the performance.

"You know, I have to talk to people. How would it be if I warned them that it was going to be very slow, and prepare them for it? Because if they don't know, they really might leave," Bernstein said. He hastily jotted a few notes on the back of an envelope and showed them to Glenn.

"Is this okay?" he said.

"Oh, it's wonderful, what a great idea," Glenn replied.

Bernstein walked onstage and addressed the audience. He ended by saying, "I have only once before, in my life, had to submit to a soloist's wholly new and incompatible concept, and that was the last time I accompanied Mr. Gould."

Soloist and orchestra earned a rousing response. The next day's headlines encapsulated the event: "Who's the Boss — Conductor or Soloist?" wondered the *New York Herald Tribune*. "Gould Gets His Knuckles Rapped" announced the *Toronto Telegram*.

※

One afternoon in very early spring of 1962, a month or so before this concert, Glenn and John Roberts drove to the Caledon Hills in Ontario. Glenn howled and conducted snatches of Brahms the entire way. He parked the car by the Credit River and the two of them, wrapped in heavy winter coats, hiked along the riverbank. Above the sound of rushing spring water, Glenn mused about the cycles of life and its shortness. When it began to rain, they returned to the car, and to the rhythmic swiping of the windshield wipers, Glenn confided that he was going to stop giving concerts. John had heard this before, of course.

But later that year, in the Shangri-La restaurant, while the *Goldberg Variations* played in the background on Bill Seto's jukebox, Glenn sipped his coffee and told John he would give his last concert in 1964. For years everyone had been telling Glenn that if he quit giving concerts, his recording career would be over. "Well, we'll see. It will be a terrific challenge," Glenn said, eyeing John and smiling. The same year, Glenn wrote his friend Humphrey Burton at the BBC in London: "I decided that when the next season is over, I shall give no more public concerts. Mind you, this is a plan I have been announcing ever since I was 18, and there is a part of my public here that does not take these pronouncements too seriously, but this time I think I really mean it."

On April 10, 1964, at the Wilshire Ebell Theatre in Los Angeles, Glenn gave his last recital in a concert hall.

Glenn Gould in his favourite place, a CBC studio. Here with the Toronto Symphony, possibly during the taping of the Beethoven bi-centennial concert, 1970. Courtesy of the Glenn Gould Estate.

10

"Once I Let My Imagination Go ..."

Glenn gripped the lectern, fixed his eyes on the Royal Conservatory of Music's graduating class of 1964, and continued his speech. "Indeed, if I could find one phrase that would sum up my wishes for you on this occasion, I think it would be devoted to convincing you of the futility of living too much by the advice of others." A few students nodded in agreement. They knew that Glenn practised what he preached, for in the face of all opinion to the contrary, he had turned away from a successful concert career, even though he had not yet publicly confirmed his retirement. When questioned, his response was, "I really would like the last half of my life to myself."

Some time after Glenn's "unofficial retirement," Arthur Rubinstein, the great Polish pianist, stared mournfully at Glenn and told him that he would give concerts again. "Think of my words," he said.

"I will, I promise," Glenn replied, "But I also promise that if this is a bet, you will lose it."

Glenn had both eyes on the future, which to him looked like a black plastic disc spinning at 33 rpm. But how would he make money? No classical musician earned a living from records alone. He was about to make a bold if not foolhardy move, at least from a financial perspective, and Glenn was not naïve about money. A few years earlier, he had formed his own company, taken part in contract negotiations, and kept accurate records of his accounts. Always fascinated by numbers and games, he played the stock market and won when others lost. The year he retired, he charged $3,500 per concert, a very respectable sum in the early 1960s, when a good car cost $2,000 and houses started at $15,000. At the time, his royalties for the *Goldberg Variations* amounted to less than $2,000. By 1962, he had recorded eighteen albums, yet he couldn't live off their royalties.

Glenn wanted money for one reason only — the freedom it could buy. In the language of the 1960s, he wanted to do "his own thing," which was to record as much as possible. But he also wanted to communicate with people directly. CBC Radio, and later CBC Television, gave him that opportunity.

On his radio show *The Art of Glenn Gould*, he entertained the weekly audience with a variety of topics. "This is Glenn Gould," he announced at the start of each segment as people at home settled into their sofas wondering what subject Glenn might dissect this time: pop singer Petula Clark, Bach's fugues, the Moog synthesizer, or any one of countless other music-related topics. Glenn felt as much at home in a radio station as he did in a recording studio. "When those first people sat glued or wired to their crystal sets, what they were really recognizing was the phenomenon of another human voice, the sheer mystery and challenge of another human voice being five blocks away and being heard," he explained.

Radio also let Glenn reveal his sense of humour. He told writer Jonathan Cott that his "most joyous moments in radio, as opposed to my most creative ones, perhaps, are those when I turn to impersonation. I was incapable of writing in a sustained humorous style until I developed an ability to portray myself pseudonymously." This was Glenn's long-winded way of saying he enjoyed role-playing. He had begun assuming roles several years earlier while writing articles for *High Fidelity* magazine. He gave free reign to his alter egos on radio and later on television, too. Theodore Slotz, based on a New York cab driver, and Sir Nigel Twitt-Thornwaite, Dean of British conductors, described by Glenn as "utterly dotty," were two of his favourites. Others included S.F. Lemming, M.D; boxer Dominic Patriano; and Myron Chianti, based on acting legend Marlon Brando. Glenn affected accents poorly, dressed up in costumes, and not only lampooned the pomposity of the music world but also scored serious points in a humorous way.

❦

The Muskeg Express wound its way along the tracks toward Fort Churchill on the southwestern shore of Hudson Bay while Glenn slumped against the window and gazed at the infinite expanse of land. As a boy he had studied maps of the North and longed to visit its vast open spaces. The North represented the ideal of complete solitude, but he had never travelled there until now. The previous evening, he had dined with Wally MacLean, a retired surveyor who had lobbed quotes from Shakespeare, Thoreau, and Kafka into their marathon eight-hour conversation. Wally's stories had inspired Glenn to return someday, but he was a poor traveller and probably wouldn't. Still, he might, for the CBC had recently proposed a project about the North and now that he was actually here, he found himself dreaming about what he might do for them.

Two years later, during Canada's Centennial Year, Glenn focused his ideas and asked five people to give their views on the North: a cynic, an enthusiast, a government budget watcher, and "someone who could represent that limitless expectation and limitless capacity for disillusionment which inevitably affects the questing spirit of those who go north seeking their future." He invited Wally MacLean, a nurse, two professors, and a federal official to talk about their experiences of the North while he recorded them.

༄

Glenn relied on his knowledge of counterpoint to develop a word score. Lorne Tulk, a recording engineer and friend with whom he had worked on an earlier documentary, assisted Glenn. The two men laboured tirelessly, often spending a hundred hours a week in the confines of the studio as night after night Glenn, his pencil cutting arabesques in the air, signalled instructions to Lorne. "Fade out the nurse and increase volume on Wally. Now, bring Wally down and bring up the federal official." Sometimes to reduce the stress, he broke into a guttural German accent and giggled as Lorne tried to follow: "Now, ziss iss ze place vhere ve haff to be zuper careful not to drown out poor Mr. MacLean."

Glenn wanted to simulate the effect of eavesdropping on several conversations at once, something he did when he ate in restaurants and tuned in on surrounding diners. He was able to select those he wanted to focus on while letting others drift off, then "tuning" them in again. Glenn called his complex idea "Contrapuntal Radio."

Their superhuman labours paid off. Critical reviews of *The Idea of North* were favourable, and the CBC invited Glenn to write and produce more documentaries. This time, he chose to make a program on Newfoundland called *The Latecomers*, which he completed in 1968. Five years later, he made the third documentary in the series, *The Quiet in the Land*. Throughout the 1970s, Glenn created numerous radio programs for CBC, including *Arnold Schoenberg: The Man Who Changed Music*; a program on Northern Ontario and popular music; *Stowkowski: A Portrait for Radio*; and *Richard Strauss: The Bourgeois Hero*. Glenn's decency, intelligence, curiosity, and enthusiasm shine in all of them as he explores his ideas of solitude and the creative process, his faith in technology, and his admiration for composers who challenged the norm.

༄

When Glenn wasn't producing documentaries, he recorded late into the night. His exceptionally acute hearing let him distinguish the tiniest differences among numerous takes. He heard nuances in tone and alterations in tempo no one else did, not even his long-time producer Andrew Kazdin with whom he had started working in 1964.

The technician might say, "Take sixteen is really good."

"Do you really think so? Hmmm. Yes, it is, isn't it? But let's do it one more time. The gigue was a bit slow," Glenn might respond before turning back to the keyboard yet again.

"I see nothing wrong in making a performance out of two hundred splices as long as the desirable result is there," Glenn

Glenn Gould

told an interviewer, and added that happiness would be "250 days a year in the recording studio." His conscientiousness paid off. By 1974, he had produced more than thirty new albums, featuring composers as different as Bach, Mozart, Beethoven, Prokofiev, Schoenberg, Grieg, and Hindemith. Each record revealed Glenn's penchant for experimentation. At times, he ignored pedal markings, strengthened bass lines, or changed tempos as the mood struck him. Once, after the first take of a Mozart sonata, Glenn dropped his hands into his lap, crouched forward and blurted, "There. That'll bug the critics."

Glenn also found time to let Bruno Monsaingeon, a French musician and filmmaker, make a documentary about him in the recording studio. At the first session, Glenn was speaking excitedly, when he leaned forward and accidentally hit the microphone gently with his head. He immediately collapsed into a chair. "My God, a concussion," he groaned, head in his hands. For the next few minutes, he fantasized about all the terrible things that would inevitably happen to him. Monsaingeon and crew stood by helplessly, worried that Glenn had really hurt himself. "Well, I know, I know, once I let my imagination go, I'm lost," he finally admitted.

Glenn recorded for Columbia's *Masterworks* series until 1975. He planned to record major works like the entire cycle of Beethoven's thirty-two piano sonatas and all sixteen Haydn suites. But he tired of the long commute to Columbia's studio in New York, and changed his venue to Eaton Auditorium. Steinway offered to move his piano, the famous CD 318, to Toronto. The instrument was dropped and severely damaged during shipping. Glenn had it repaired, but was never satisfied with its sound again. On the advice of jazz pianist Bill Evans, he purchased a Yamaha grand.

About this time, a new person came into Glenn's life. Ray Roberts was only thirty-one when Glenn offered him part-time work. Ray modestly described himself as a "glorified gofer," and for the first while lugged equipment back and forth between Glenn's apartment and Eaton Auditorium. Glenn came to consider Ray a good friend and relied on him greatly for all kinds of assistance and support.

Ray must have been amused by his friend's daily routine, which rarely varied. If Glenn wasn't at the microphone late into the night, he sat up editing or writing until the wee small hours. The apartment, like the cottage, was always messy. Ketchup bottles, Arrowroot cookie boxes, empty milk cartons, records, pens, newspapers, books, hotel keys, clothes, pads of foolscap — the minutiae of his life littered the place. If he wasn't working, he doodled on scraps of paper, played word games, solved puzzles, or made up lists of questions about subjects of interest to him. Every night around 11:00 p.m., Glenn picked up the telephone and called whoever came to mind. The phone was Glenn's link to the world, and it cost him hundreds of dollars monthly. "I live by long distance," he said.

Late one evening, Robert Silverman, editor of *The Piano Quarterly*, answered the phone. A torrent of words poured from the receiver. At least Glenn wasn't playing an entire orchestral score on the piano and screeching the parts his fingers couldn't play. Three hours later Silverman fell asleep on the floor, phone still to his ear. His son kicked him in the foot. "Dad, are you awake? Are you talking to someone?" Both could hear Glenn gleefully nattering away. Then "click," and the line was silent.

Glenn Gould

Glenn emerged from his apartment a few minutes later, went to the parking lot and fired up "Longfellow," his black Lincoln town car. The Chevrolet Monte Carlo, "Lance" waited in the adjacent spot. His cars were like comfortable cocoons to him whereas to others they were dangerous missiles. Speeding fines cost him a small fortune and a few court appearances.

Glenn pulled out, narrowly missing the car behind him. It wouldn't be the first time he had hit a car, skidded into a curb, or plowed into a snowbank. He turned onto St. Clair Avenue ready for a cruise through Toronto's late night streets, or perhaps a drive into the surrounding countryside. Several hours later, he parked and entered an all-night diner and ordered scrambled eggs, toast, and coffee, which he drank with a heavy dose of powdered creamer. He picked at his food, eavesdropped on the next booth, and scanned the stock market page in the *Toronto Star*. Two hours later he left and drove home in the morning traffic. That afternoon, he woke up and religiously called his stockbroker before dressing in his customary black, grey, or blue while the radio and television blared in the background.

Glenn found solitude in the heart of a large, busy city. He became known as the recluse of St. Clair Avenue, although he really wasn't. He had many friends like John Roberts, Peter Ostwald, and Ray Roberts. He no longer saw Robert Fulford because their friendship had cooled some years earlier, but no one knew why. Glenn worked with talented people like producer Andrew Kazdin and recording engineer Lorne Tulk, and he had many acquaintances. A sweet man who loved young people, Glenn took neighbours' children for long walks at the cottage, and never patronized them. Sometimes he visited John Roberts and entertained his children with bedtime stories. He would go on and on until John or his wife stopped him so the youngsters could finally go to sleep. Glenn adored animals and frequently dragged stray dogs into the recording studio where he fed them biscuits.

Fans could be nosy. Some tampered with his mail; others, hoping to catch sight of him, loitered around the building. One afternoon, Glenn was lost in a score when the buzzer sounded. Instead of answering, he phoned Marilyn Keckes, the superintendent. Marilyn used to sit on the roof underneath the moon and stars after she had finished cleaning and secretly listen to Glenn play. "Marilyn. Glenn. There's someone knocking on my door. Could you see what they want?" he said and hung up.

Although he was now in his forties, Glenn was still a bachelor. Many women pestered him with love letters, and a few dropped by the apartment in hope of hearing him practise. But he didn't have a girlfriend; at least no one was completely certain if he did because he was so very private about his romantic life. "Music is *my* ecstasy," he said teasingly.

People gossiped and the rumours amused him, for Glenn understood that the less he said, the more people would talk about him, and he loved being the centre of attention. He had a few flings and confessed to Ray Roberts about "a torrid affair in his twenties" with an unnamed woman. He engaged in one serious romance with Cornelia Foss, a beautiful and talented artist who was married to Lukas Foss, a famous pianist and conductor. Cornelia left her husband and moved to Toronto to be close to Glenn. But their romance eventually ended and Cornelia returned to the United States. Glenn was heartbroken. He drove to the Hamptons, where the Fosses lived, to persuade her to come back. After a painful conversation, he came home alone.

For some time after, he phoned Cornelia almost nightly until she finally persuaded him to stop.

Glenn's bachelor lifestyle suited him perfectly, but the years of physical abuse — poor eating habits, late nights, and stress — began to show. He looked weary and haggard much of the time, and friends worried about his dependence on medication. Glenn shrugged off their concerns. "Most of my earlier illnesses were psychosomatic — a sheer protest against my regimen," he told them even though he still visited doctors regularly with complaints about various ailments, ingested too many pills, and obsessed about catching germs. As always, however, he had plans for many new projects.

11

One of the God-People

One day in July of 1975, as Bert Gould walked up the steps to his house, Florence opened the door, and to his horror, she started to collapse in front of him. He managed to catch her before she hit the floor. An ambulance rushed her to East General Hospital. Glenn had his mother transferred to Toronto General Hospital, where she lay in coma for a few days. Florence had suffered a stroke. Glenn was sick with worry and hounded the doctors daily by phone, but he wouldn't set foot in the hospital because he was terrified of germs. Florence regained consciousness briefly before she died, and Glenn spoke to her on the phone.

All these years she had been the person closest to him. No one could replace her. Glenn's friends worried about him. Lorne Tulk saw how unfocused Glenn was the week after his mother's death. His powers of concentration were legendary, but now,

ACTRA award nomination for the best documentary writer or public affairs writer for television, honouring Cities: Glenn Gould's Toronto. *February, 1980. Courtesy of the Glenn Gould Estate.*

nothing gelled because he was stricken with grief. He endured his pain in silence. In honour of Florence's memory, he gave a eulogy in which he says of his mother that she "was a woman of tremendous faith and, wherever she went, she strove to instill that faith in others."

Glenn grew even more inward-looking and increasingly relied on Jessie for solace. He reached out to her frequently for comfort and to share his thoughts. Jessie once said, "After his mother's death he phoned and he said that he never knew what the loving support of a family could be until that time. He first became aware of it then."

*

Soon after Florence's death, Glenn was diagnosed with high blood pressure and immediately began to obsess about it. In a daily, sometimes hourly ritual, he sat at the table covered with pads of paper, pens, rolled up his sleeves, and wound the band of one three blood pressure gauges around his bicep. He squeezed the bulb and watched the mercury shoot up then fall, then repeated the same steps with the other gauges and recorded and compared all the readings. He fretted about his heart and his general health. Among other ailments, he complained of poor circulation, sore throats, and chest pains, and he kept detailed records of these as well. His diet didn't help. "He did zero exercise and he ate scrambled eggs every damn day," Ray Roberts said.

Glenn pestered numerous doctors, obtained prescriptions from each of them, and crammed vials of pills into his medicine cabinet. He consulted books on pharmacology and made up long lists of questions for his doctors. Journals filled with detailed observations about his body were strewn about his apartment. "Chest, periodic tightness," one entry reads. "Some finger pains equivalent to first uric acid finding," another states. He studied his hand movements and brooded darkly on various pains in his arms and back. In 1977, he made a sombre diary entry that reads, "lack of coordination was noticed in June." He was experiencing problems similar to the ones he had noticed years earlier when the Steinway technician had touched his shoulder. Glenn spent some time trying to solve the problem, but was never happy with his piano playing again.

※

Throughout the 1970s, Glenn kept up his insane schedule of recording and television work. He also collaborated with the famous violinist Yehudi Menuhin on the latter's *Music of Man* series and threw himself into his radio documentary on Richard Strauss, a composer who according to Glenn "makes richer his own time by not being of it."

Opportunities also opened up for composing for films. Glenn had not fulfilled his early promise as a composer and felt guilty about his failure. He joked about his Opus 2, meaning his second work after the String Quartet, op. 1, which he had written at the cottage back in the 1950s. Since then, he had started and stopped his Opus 2 many times.

Now he could put his talent to use and compose soundtracks. He loved the peaceful oblivion of movies theatres where he could give himself up to the fascinating play of light and sound. In 1971, he selected bits from his records and composed the continuity for the soundtrack to the film *Slaughterhouse-Five*, based on Kurt Vonnegut's novel of the same name.

He also continued to write. He had always thought of himself as a writer, and had often said that someday he might author a novel. He never did. For someone so in tune with technology, Glenn preferred his black ballpoints to a typewriter. He wrote essays for magazines like *High Fidelity* and *The Piano Quarterly*, and often succumbed to his love of big words and long, puffy sentences. Topics ranged from Bach to popular music and from technology to the nature of music competitions. One essay, "We Who Are About to Be Disqualified Salute You," argues that superbly gifted musicians who possess a unique vision are the ones who should win music competitions; instead, it's the ones who conform to accepted taste who all too often walk off with first prize. Glenn's essays range in quality from brilliant to humorous to pompous and sometimes all three at once. These essays later were collected and published in *The Glenn Gould Reader*.

On a misty dawn in 1978, Glenn stood in the Toronto Zoo, a camera recording his gestures as he sang Gustav Mahler's *St. Anthony's Sermon to the Fishes* to the bored elephants for a scene in a documentary about Toronto. Some time earlier, John McGreevy of the CBC had asked Glenn to write a script about the city and to be the on-camera tour guide. Glenn was eager to do it, for he knew the city well, or so he thought. But by this time, Toronto had transformed into a cosmopolitan centre, a city of immigrants who proudly displayed their cultures everywhere and of suburbs that engulfed the surrounding countryside with tracts of housing and ever-proliferating malls. Glenn had ignored this slow metamorphosis and still thought of Toronto as it was in the good old days when the vast majority of the people were WASP and everything was closed on Sundays. While he was filming the documentary, he had fun showing off the new city hall, the Ontario Science Centre, Kensington Market, and other highlights. At one point in the new Eaton Centre, which he had never visited, he exclaims good-naturedly: "It's absurd! I don't believe it."

*

Glenn read over the draft of a letter to his father, crumpled it, and pitched it on the floor. The tone simply wasn't right. He had started so many of these during the past several months ever since Bert had asked him to be his best man at his wedding to Vera Dobson, an old friend of the family. Their relationship had been getting serious while Glenn had been busy with his career.

He look at the pad where he had written some notes and read one aloud: "my point is that not sure it's approp[riate] for person of your age to change their spots so radically, if indeed, that's what you're doing." He sighed, combed his fingers through his hair, and started yet another draft. The romance displeased him because he could not tolerate the idea that Bert might replace Florence. Bert had grieved for a long time after his wife's death, and Glenn had tried to console him even though they were never close. Glenn scanned over his scribbles and scrunched up the paper. He grabbed the phone and began to pace the room as the cord dragged across the piles of manuscripts and records lying on the floor. When Bert answered, Glenn wished him and Vera well but declined to attend the wedding because his memory of Florence was too strong, and he would not allow anyone to diminish it.

Glenn was wrestling with other decisions as well. One day in 1979, he called Jonathan Cott, who was interviewing him for a book. "You know, in three years I'll be fifty, and I've been thinking that that would be a good year for me to give up making piano recordings," Glenn said. Was he kidding? No one knew. Only one thing was certain: Glenn had many ambitions as yet unrealized. During the past ten years, his desire to be a conductor had intensified, maybe in part spurred on by his never-ending physical problems while playing piano.

Perhaps Glenn would have given up the piano all together and taken up the baton full time at this point, but in 1981, he went back to the studio to re-record and to film the *Goldberg Variations* because studio technology had greatly improved since 1955, the year he made his first record for Columbia. He also wanted to reinterpret several of the variations. For his second recording, Glenn returned to Columbia's New York studio, and for six days in April and May of 1981, he allowed Bruno Monsaingeon to film the sessions.

Glenn was his usual demanding self at these sessions. Fussy as ever about the editing process, he brought the master tapes back to Toronto to edit on his own equipment. The result was a landmark recording and film. Upon its release, the new *Goldberg Variations* provided music lovers with years of endless debate about which version was better — the youthful one with its quicker tempos or the middle-aged version, which many think more meditative. The film of the recording session shows Glenn in middle age: his face is puffy, the skin pale and blotchy, and his posture is noticeably more stooped.

In 1982, Glenn was asked to compose the music for *The Wars*, a film based on Canadian author Timothy Findley's novel of the same name. Findley admired Glenn and called him one of the "god-people." Glenn's only reservation was that the film had a dead horse in it. "I know the horse is dead, but if it was killed for the film, I couldn't work on it," he told Richard Neilson, one of the producers.

"I think we got him from an abattoir, where they kill old horses for horsemeat," Neilson assured him.

"Well, fine, then we'll do it," Glenn replied and also agreed to meet the author to view and discuss the film.

Findley waited for Glenn in the screening room. Suddenly, he heard a slop, slop, slop sound and Glenn entered, wearing galoshes. They shook hands and settled back to screen the film Glenn was to score. Findley was shocked by his appearance and said after the screening, "He's sick — he's really ill. He looked ill, because the colour of his skin was so alarming. And his hair looked dead. It really had that awful look of someone who's been ill in a very major way, so that their hair dies. And it looked like that — it looked like dead hair."

Despite his poor health, Glenn was eager to do this project, for he admired the book. Glenn chose not to compose new music but to arrange existing compositions, with the exception of a few cello and bass passages. He created a collage that included works by other composers, some hymns, a few popular songs, and snatches of his own piano performances taken from records. He personally edited and mixed the soundtrack, which upon completion was "exquisite." People did wonder, though, why he had once again passed up an opportunity to compose something entirely new.

Glenn also had many other ideas for the future, and even fantasized about building an animal shelter in the Arctic. "And guess who was going to be the manager," Ray Roberts said. Glenn also had plans for Jessie. "When we get old and senile," he told his cousin, "I'll buy a house, and you can have the bottom floor, and I'll have the top floor." Some of these plans were probably tongue-in-cheek but others weren't.

A Musical Force

Glenn decided that now was definitely the time to get serious about conducting. He had tried before, but hadn't pursued it. "Conductors live a long time, you know. It'll give me several more years to look forward to," he joked. Glenn drew up a list of potential works, important compositions by composers like Brahms and Beethoven, whose demanding scores were usually tackled only by seasoned maestros. Glenn, however, believed he was up to the challenge even though he lacked formal training.

On April Fools Day of 1982, Jon Klibonoff, a young pianist in New York, answered his phone and heard a voice that sounded like a Brooklyn cabbie, but was really Glenn doing his Theodore Slotz impersonation. Jon was floored. He had never met Glenn. They chatted for a few minutes, and Glenn said, "I'll bet you come from about forty-five minutes west of the Lincoln Tunnel."

"I do. What a fantastic ear," Jon replied, amazed that Glenn could guess where he lived so accurately simply by his accent. Glenn suddenly began to sing the orchestral *tutti* section of the concerto he wanted Jon to play. Klibonoff joined in and they screeched through the entire first movement.

Later that month, Jon waited in the empty theatre in Hamilton for Glenn and the Hamilton Philharmonic when a capped and coated figure sauntered in. "You must be Jon," Glenn said. They shook hands and immediately got to work at the piano.

When the musicians arrived, Glenn stepped onto the podium and gave the downbeat to Beethoven's Piano Concerto no. 2 in B-flat Major, op. 19. Conducting is a bit like dancing: every move has meaning. It takes a lot of experience to be comfortable on the podium. Glenn had a great deal of trouble at first, and the musicians found his meandering hands difficult to follow, especially in the second movement, which Glenn took at a very slow tempo. But all of them responded to his enthusiasm and encouragement and gave him everything they had. Glenn was delighted with their cooperation and wanted to rehearse well into the night, but union rules forbade it.

In July 1982, Glenn recorded Richard Wagner's *Siegfried Idyll* with a chamber group. He arrived at the session carrying a green garbage bag stuffed with scores, notepads, and other items. The rehearsal dragged on for hours. To relieve the monotony Glenn devised a game to name the ensemble. "How about Gould's Ghouls," a violist called out. "The Siegried Idyleirs," another offered. "The Academy of St. Lawrence in the Market," Glenn suggested, a takeoff on the Academy of St. Martin in the Fields, a well-known British ensemble group specializing in Baroque music. Afterwards, clarinetist Timothy Maloney praised the fledgling conductor: "He did his best to make us feel like partners in the endeavour rather than as sidemen to the maestro."

The future for Glenn's newest venture into music making looked promising. On September 25, 1982, Glenn turned fifty. Friends arranged a birthday party, but he didn't feel well enough to attend. Instead, he called a few people and chatted. Bert and Vera dropped by with some cookies.

Two days later, Glenn woke up and felt something was wrong. He went to the bathroom, sat down, and fell asleep. When he woke, he suspected he had suffered a stroke because his speech was slurred and his left arm was numb. He phoned Ray Roberts, who rushed over and was stunned when Glenn himself opened the door. The two phoned several doctors for a diagnosis because Glenn wouldn't hear of going to the hospital. Ray finally guided him out of the room and into the Lincoln, then drove him to Toronto General, where the doctors diagnosed a stroke.

Jessie Greig arrived shortly after, but was allowed to stay only a few minutes. Glenn gripped her hand tightly while she sat beside him. "I know you're terribly ill, but we Greigs are fighters, you know," she said.

"Yes, but it's too late, now. It's just too late," Glenn said.

Some time later, Bert came and spoke to his unconscious son. Glenn's arm came up and began to wave as if he were conducting. Two days later, he suffered another stroke. On October 4, 1982, Glenn Gould died, and Canada began to mourn.

Glenn Gould during CBC publicity shoot for The Idea of North. *Courtesy of the Glenn Gould Estate.*

Epilogue

Elusive Voyager

A young woman walks among the headstones in Toronto's Mount Pleasant Cemetery. She could be from Canada or any one of a dozen other countries where Glenn's reputation has grown in the years since his death. Forehead creased in thought, she pauses to glance up at the grey clouds in the late November sky. The day is cold and damp, and she hugs herself for warmth, zips her jacket, and adjusts her headphones before resuming her slow pace. Sony's 2002 reissue of the 1955 and 1982 *Goldberg Variations* is her constant companion, and she has listened to it countless times, always surprised at the pulsing relentless energy of Glenn's playing. Whenever she hears it, she thinks of a flame encased in ice. She smiles as she thinks of the film *Thirty-two Short Films About Glenn Gould*. One of her favourite scenes shows Glenn, as portrayed by Colm Feore, standing on the shore of a frozen lake. He is dressed in long overcoat, cap, scarf, and gloves. He turns and begins to walk toward the white horizon stretching to infinity.

Like so many of his fans, she has read about Glenn and knows that during his lifetime he received The Harriet Cohen Bach Medal, the Canada Council's Molson Prize, the Canadian Music Council Medal, and the *Diplôme d'honneur* from the Canadian Conference of the Arts. The years since his death have only increased his stature and added to his mystery. He was inducted into the Canadian Music Hall of Fame and the National Academy of Recording Arts and Sciences. Many books and articles were and continue to be written about him. The CBC made a documentary about him: *Glenn Gould: A Portrait*. His 1982 recording of the *Goldberg Variations* won two GRAMMY awards, a JUNO award, and a Gold Disc from the Canadian Recording Industry.

A promising young pianist, she dreams of such success for herself, but on this day, she is here in this lonely cemetery to pay homage to a musician who died before she was born, but whose music has kept her company for years. She admires Glenn's life as much as she envies his fluid, delicate technique. Art was the essence of his being, and he never wavered in his commitment to it. For Glenn, music was about the human soul and its longing for expression. He beckoned to people and invited them to take part in his music making, to join in the act of creation with him. He favoured some composers and criticized others. He provoked, teased, and even clowned around, but he always made people think about music and musicians.

At last she spots the Gould family plot and the simple granite stone engraved with Glenn's name, year of birth and death, and the outline of a grand piano. Inscribed along the bottom are the first three measures of the "Aria" from the *Goldberg Variations*.

Upon seeing them, she nods her head as if to say "Yes, of course. So it must be."

As she stands at his grave, somewhere overhead many billions of kilometres from Earth, the twin spacecraft *Voyager 1* and *Voyager 2* continue a journey that began in the late seventies. Aboard, they carry time capsules with recorded sounds of planet Earth and greetings in different languages. One of those sounds is of Glenn Gould playing Bach's Prelude and Fugue in C Major from Book One of *The Well-Tempered Clavier* by J.S. Bach. "Surely," the young woman thinks, "no finer introduction to the human race is possible."

Chronology of Glenn Gould (1932–1982)

Compiled by Rhonda Bailey

Gould and His Times

1932
On September 25, Glenn Herbert Gould is born in Toronto at the home of his parents, Florence Emma Gould (née Greig), a piano and voice teacher, and Russell Herbert (Bert) Gould, a furrier.

1935
The Goulds discover that Glenn is gifted with perfect pitch.

Florence Gould is Glenn's first piano teacher. He receives piano lessons from his mother until he is ten years old.

Canada and the World

1932
Franklin Delano Roosevelt is elected president of the United States (U.S.)

During the Great Depression, over 30 million people are unemployed worldwide.

1933
In Germany, composer Paul Hindemith begins work on the opera *Mathis der Maler (Matthias the Painter)*.

1935
In Canada, the On to Ottawa Trek of men from unemployment relief camps is stopped in Regina by the RCMP; a riot leaves one dead and hundreds injured.

Liberal William Lyon Mackenzie

Gould and His Times

Canada and the World

King defeats R.B. Bennett to become prime minister of Canada. Two new parties, the CCF and Social Credit, appear in Parliament.

Austrian-born pianist Arthur Schnabel finishes recording the thirty-two Beethoven sonatas. This is the first recording of the complete set of Beethoven sonatas.

1936
In Great Britain, King George VI succeeds his brother, Edward VIII, who has abdicated in order to marry Wallis Simpson, an American divorcée.

The British Broadcasting Corporation (BBC) inaugurates television service.

Nazi Germany and Fascist Italy form an alliance.

Austrian-born composer Arnold Schoenberg, founder of the twelve-tone technique of composition, has moved to the U.S. and begins teaching at UCLA.

Arthur Schnabel is touring and performing concerts regularly in the U.S.

A Musical Force

Gould and His Times

Canada and the World

In Canada, the Canadian Broadcasting Corporation (CBC), a crown corporation, is created.

1938
On June 5 at the Uxbridge United Church, Gould gives his first public performance on piano.

The Goulds hire a private tutor for Glenn, who takes Grade 1 at home.

Glenn hears Polish-born pianist Josef Hofmann give a recital in Toronto's Massey Hall.

1939
In Grade 2, he attends Williamson Road Public School.

1938
Hitler marches into Austria; Britain tries to appease Germany at Munich.

In the U.S. a new dance craze, the Jitterbug, sweeps the country. The Swing Era begins, led by Benny Goodman and his band.

1939
The National Film Board of Canada (NFB) is created. John Grierson becomes Government Film Commissioner.

The Second World War begins on September 1 with Germany's invasion of Poland. Canada declares war on Germany on September 7. The U.S. is officially neutral.

Hollywood blockbusters *Gone With the Wind* and *The Wizard of Oz* entertain audiences.

Gould and His Times

1940
Gould earns first class honours in Grade 3 piano in his first examination at the Toronto Conservatory of Music (TCM).

He begins to study music theory with Leo Smith at TCM.

1941
In Grade 4 at Williamson Road Public School Gould becomes friends with Robert Fulford; the two boys spend hours playing together or listening to CBC Radio reports from the war front.

Canada and the World

1940
Winston Churchill becomes prime minister of Great Britain.

Italy enters the war alongside its ally, Germany.

The NFB's monthly theatrical newsreel series, *Canada Carries On*, circulates in 800 Canadian cinemas during the war.

Composer Paul Hindemith has immigrated to the U.S. and begins teaching theory of music at Yale University.

Russian-born classical pianist Vladimir Horowitz also settles in the U.S.

1941
On December 7, Japan bombs Pearl Harbor; the U.S., Canada, and Britain declare war on Japan.

Canada uses the War Measures Act to forcibly move Canadian citizens of Japanese descent away from the Pacific Coast.

The CBC and Radio-Canada launch their News Service.

Sir Frederick Banting dies in a plane crash in Newfoundland.

A Musical Force

Gould and His Times

1942
Gould begins organ lessons with Frederic K. Silvester at the TCM. He also studies theory with Leo Smith.

During the summer he falls and injures his back at the Gould family cottage at Lake Simcoe.

1943
Gould begins piano lessons with Chilean-born concert pianist and teacher Alberto Guerrero.

1944
In February Gould competes in the First Annual Kiwanis Music Festival and wins first prize in the piano trophy competition.

Canada and the World

Arnold Schoenberg becomes an American citizen.

1942
In a plebiscite, the majority of Canadians vote for conscription, although the opposite result is obtained in the province of Quebec,

Canada provides the major assault force (5000 troops) for Allied landings at the port of Dieppe, France. The raid fails, and Canadian troops suffer heavy losses.

In the U.S., the Manhattan Project of atomic research to develop a nuclear weapon begins.

1943
In the Canadian War Records project, the government of Canada hires thirty-one official war artists to paint the activities of the Canadian armed forces during the Second World War.

1944
In the U.S., President Roosevelt dies and Harry S. Truman succeeds him.

On June 6, Allied forces land on the Normandy beaches of France in the D-Day invasion;

133

Glenn Gould

Gould and His Times

Canada and the World

the Canadian Army again suffers heavy losses in the Battle of Normandy.

1945
On March 10, Gould plays on the radio for the first time, on the program Kiwanis Festival Winners, which is aired by station CFRB.

At the Kiwanis Music Festival, he is awarded the Gordon Thompson Scholarship.

In June he passes his piano examination for the TCM Associateship; he is the youngest student ever to earn the coveted diploma.

In September he begins attending Malvern Collegiate Institute.

Jessie Greig, Glenn's eighteen-year-old cousin, comes to live with the Gould family while she attends teacher's college in Toronto.

In December he gives his first public recital on organ at Eaton Auditorium in downtown Toronto.

1945
In May, Canadians liberate western Holland; Germany's surrender on May 7 ends the war in Europe. The Nazi death camps are discovered.

In August, the U.S. drops two atomic bombs on Japan. On September 2, Japan surrenders. The Second World War ends.

The United Nations (UN) is founded to maintain peace in the world and to protect the fundamental rights of man.

U.S. President Roosevelt dies and is succeeded by Harry Truman.

Arthur Schnabel becomes an American citizen.

A Musical Force

Gould and His Times

1946
On May 8 at Massey Hall, Gould debuts with the Toronto Conservatory Symphony Orchestra.

Walter Homburger approaches Bert and Florence Gould and offers to manage their son.

In October Gould receives the TCM Associate Diploma.

1947
On January 14 and 15, Gould debuts with the Toronto Symphony Orchestra at Massey Hall. He plays the Piano Concerto no. 4 in G Major, op. 58 by Beethoven. The conductor is Bernard Heinze.

On April 10, he gives a concert at the Toronto Conservatory of Music. He then appears at various venues around Toronto and in nearby towns. His reputation grows.

Walter Homburger arranges for Gould to play his first public solo piano recital, an International Artists Series recital at Eaton Auditorium, Toronto.

Canada and the World

1946
In a speech, Winston Churchill, former prime minister of Britain, uses the term "Iron Curtain" to describe the developing Cold War between the Eastern bloc and the West.

Polish-born classical pianist Arthur Rubenstein becomes an American citizen.

American classical pianist Gary Graffman makes his solo debut, with Eugene Ormandy and the Philadelphia Symphony Orchestra.

1947
In Canada, the Massey-Levesque Royal Commission on the Arts leads to federal funding of the arts to help build and sustain national culture.

British India is granted independence by the United Kingdom and is partitioned into two sovereign states, India and Pakistan.

Glenn Gould

Gould and His Times

1948
Gould composes his *Sonata for Piano*. This is his first major composition.

Guerrero introduces his pupil to the modern compositions of Arnold Schoenberg. Inspired after hearing Schoenberg and other contemporary composers, Gould immerses himself in learning about contemporary compositional technique.

1949
Gould plays a suite of his own music as an overture to the Malvern Collegiate Institute's production of *Twelfth Night*.

Canada and the World

1948
Mackenzie King retires and is succeeded as prime minister of Canada by Louis Saint-Laurent.

In India, spiritual and political leader Mahatma Ghandi is assassinated.

A new Jewish state called the State of Israel is formally established.

1949
Canada is one of the founders of the North Atlantic Treaty Organization (NATO).

Newfoundland joins Confederation as Canada's tenth province.

Mao Zedong proclaims the People's Republic of China.

In South Africa, apartheid is implemented.

Canadian pianist Oscar Peterson makes a brief guest appearance at Carnegie Hall in New York, which launches his long and distinguished international jazz career.

A Musical Force

Gould and His Times

1950
On February 12, Gould performs at the University of Toronto's Sunday Evening Concert.

He performs at the University of Western Ontario in London on November 26. This is his first major performance outside his hometown of Toronto.

He composes his second major work, *Sonata for Bassoon and Piano*.

On December 24, he plays piano on CBC Radio. This is his radio debut for the Canadian Broadcasting Corporation, and marks the beginning of a long relationship with the CBC.

Gould's friend Robert Fulford leaves high school to work as a sports writer for the *Globe and Mail*.

1951
On tour in western Canada, Gould performs with the Vancouver Symphony Orchestra on October 28 at the Orpheum Theatre. On November 7, he plays for the Calgary Women's Musical Club.

Canada and the World

1950
The Korean War begins when Communist North Korea invades South Korea. UN troops intervene under the command of American General Douglas MacArthur.

China occupies Tibet.

Former Canadian prime minister Mackenzie King dies.

1951
Princess Elizabeth makes her first royal visit to Canada with her husband Prince Philip, Duke of Edinburgh.

The Massey Commission on Arts, Letters, and Sciences publishes its report, which advocates federal support of the arts in Canada.

137

Glenn Gould

Gould and His Times

Canada and the World

Composer Arnold Schoenberg dies in Los Angeles, CA.

Allied occupation of Germany ends.

1952
Gould quits his studies with Alberto Guerrero.

He leaves Malvern Collegiate without matriculating. He leaves Toronto and goes to live at the cottage on Lake Simcoe.

Gould and Robert Fulford form New Music Associates. They produce three concerts between 1952 and 1954.

On September 8, Gould performs on CBC-TV. He is the first pianist in Canada to do so.

1952
King George VI of Britain dies and is succeeded by his daughter, who becomes Queen Elizabeth II.

Dwight D. Eisenhower becomes U.S. president.

The Canadian Broadcasting Corporation inaugurates broadcast television.

1953
Gould performs at the Stratford Festival for the first time.

He gives his first recital in eastern Canada in the St. John High School Auditorium, St. John, New Brunswick.

He makes his first commercial record.

1953
In the Union of Soviet Socialist Republics (U.S.S.R.), Nikita Khrushchev succeeds Joseph Stalin as First Secretary of the Communist Party.

The Korean War ends.

Vladimir Horowitz retires from the concert stage and does not return for twelve years.

A Musical Force

Gould and His Times

1954
The third concert produced by New Music Associates is scheduled for October 15, the night Hurricane Hazel hits Toronto.

On December 14, Gould appears with the Montreal Symphony Orchestra at Plateau Hall, Montreal.

1955
Gould gives two recitals in the U.S., the first on January 2 at the Phillips Gallery in Washington, D.C.; the second his New York debut on January 11 at Town Hall in New York.

On January 12, he signs an exclusive recording contract with Columbia Records.

He finishes composing his String Quartet, Opus 1.

1956
Glenn Gould's recording of the *Goldberg Variations* is released by Columbia Records. He becomes a celebrity.

On March 15 he plays with the Detroit Symphony Orchestra. This is his first American appearance with an orchestra.

Canada and the World

1954
In Canada, Hurricane Hazel strikes Toronto on October 15, killing 81 people and leaving 1,896 families homeless.

1955
The Warsaw Pact unites the Eastern Bloc countries militarily.

In Canada, hockey fans riot at the Montreal Forum when Quebec hockey hero Maurice ("Rocket") Richard is suspended by National Hockey League president Clarence Campbell.

1956
In the Middle East, Egypt announces the nationalization of the Suez Canal. Israel attacks Egypt. French and British troops land in Suez to protect the canal.

In Hungary on October 23, insurrection occurs in Budapest. Soviet troops intervene.

Glenn Gould

Gould and His Times

In the fall he goes on a tour of Canada and the U.S.

1957

On January 26 in Carnegie Hall, Gould debuts with the New York Philharmonic Orchestra under the baton of Leonard Bernstein.

On March 28, he performs with the Cleveland Orchestra.

On May 3, he embarks on his first overseas tour. He is the first North American pianist and first Canadian musician to perform in the U.S.S.R.

On May 7, he performs in the Great Hall of the Moscow State Conservatory. On May 8 and May 11 his concerts at Tchaikovsky Hall are sold out.

On May 12, he gives a talk and recital at the Moscow State Conservatory, "Music in the West." He is determined to introduce Russians to modern music.

Canada and the World

Canadian Lester B. Pearson proposes a UN peacekeeping force as a means of solving the Suez Crisis.

In the U.S., Elvis Presley has five #1 hit songs, makes his first national TV appearances, and becomes a cultural icon —"the King of Rock 'n' Roll."

1957

The U.S.S.R. launches Sputnik I and II, the first artificial earth satellites.

Lester B. Pearson is awarded the Nobel Peace Prize for his efforts during the Suez Crisis.

Conservative John G. Diefenbaker is elected prime minister of Canada.

The Canada Council for the Arts is founded.

Leonard Bernstein becomes sole conductor of the New York Philharmonic Orchestra. He is the first American-born holder of the post.

A Musical Force

Gould and His Times

On May 14 and 16, Gould repeats his Moscow concert programs in Leningrad at Bolshoi Hall. On May 18, he plays again at the Bolshoi Hall with the Leningrad Philharmonic Orchestra to a packed hall with 1,100 standees.

On May 24, 25, and 26 he performs in West Berlin with the Berlin Philharmonic Orchestra, conducted by Herbert von Karajan. He repeats his lecture-recital "Music in the West" at the conservatory in Leningrad.

On June 7, he appears at the Vienna Festival in Austria. Like the other concerts on this tour, his Vienna concert is a triumph.

Between August and December, he performs concerts in various North American cities.

1958
In the spring Gould tours and performs in various cities in the U.S. and Canada. In July, he performs three concerts at the inaugural Vancouver International Festival.

From August until December, he tours Austria, Sweden, West Germany, Italy, and Israel. In Israel, he gives eleven concerts in eighteen days.

Canada and the World

1958
Nikita Khruschev becomes Chairman of the Council of Ministers in the U.S.S.R.

In Cuba, Communist rebel Fidel Castro leads a guerrilla war against the regime of General Batista.

Twenty-three-year-old American pianist Van Cliburn wins the

141

Glenn Gould

Gould and His Times

On August 25, he performs at the Brussels World Fair in Belgium in the Canada Day concert.

1959
In February, Gould is awarded the Harriet Cohen Bach Medal.

Between May 20 and June 5, he gives five concerts in Great Britain, performing with the London Symphony Orchestra. He also gives two recitals for the BBC.

On August 31, he performs with the Philharmonia Orchestra at the Lucerne Festival in Switzerland. This will be his last concert in Europe.

In November, Alberto Guerrero dies.

Gould moves into two suites at the Windsor Arms hotel, then briefly leases a mansion called Donchery.

1960
Gould acquires the six-room penthouse apartment on St. Clair Avenue West in Toronto that will be his home for the rest of his life.

Canada and the World

first International Tchaikovsky Competition in Moscow.

1959
Fidel Castro takes power in Cuba when Batista flees the country.

In France, Charles De Gaulle is proclaimed president of the Fifth Republic.

Queen Elizabeth II and U.S. president Dwight D. Eisenhower officially open the St. Lawrence Seaway.

1960
John F. Kennedy becomes president of the U.S.

In Quebec, following the death of Maurice Duplessis, the Quiet Revolution begins.

A Musical Force

Gould and His Times

He finds his ideal instrument in the famous Steinway piano CD 318.

A shoulder injury causes Gould to cancel concerts in the spring. In the summer season, he appears at the Vancouver International Festival and the Stratford Festival.

The National Film Board releases two documentary films, *Glenn Gould: On the Record* and *Glenn Gould: Off the Record*.

1961
Gould becomes one of the directors of music at the Stratford Shakespearean Festival. He performs three concerts at Stratford in the 1961 season.

In August he performs twice at the Vancouver International Festival. The second show is broadcast on CBC-TV.

He gives concerts in Montreal and in cities across the U.S.

Canada and the World

1961
The construction of the Berlin Wall divides the Eastern Bloc from Western Europe and intensifies the Cold War.

Soviet astronaut Yuri Gagarin becomes the first human being to fly in space.

The U.S. enters the Vietnam War.

On April 17, Cuban exiles attempt an unsuccessful invasion of Cuba at the Bay of Pigs.

Glenn Gould

Gould and His Times

1962
Gould makes several broadcasts on CBC, including a documentary he writes and hosts, "Arnold Schoenberg: The Man Who Changed Music"

He writes the essay "Let's Ban Applause."

At Carnegie Hall, conductor Leonard Bernstein of the New York Philharmonic publicly disagrees with Gould's slow performance of the Brahms Concerto in D Minor. *New York Times* music critic Harold Schonberg publishes a malevolent and hurtful review. Other newspaper reviews also criticize Gould harshly.

Gould's boyhood friend Robert Fulford becomes editor of *Macleans* magazine, a position he holds for two years.

1963
On March 4, CBC-TV broadcasts Gould's documentary *The Anatomy of the Fugue*.

On April 22, Gould gives the Corbett Music Lecture, *Arnold Schoenberg: A Perspective*, at the University of Cincinnati, Cincinnati, Ohio.

Canada and the World

1962
A standoff between John F. Kennedy and Nikita Khrushchev over Soviet missiles in Cuba brings the world to the brink of nuclear war.

Canadian jazz pianist Oscar Peterson composes "Hymn to Freedom," which the Oscar Peterson Trio records for the first time on the album *Night Train*.

Russian-American pianist Vladimir Horowitz makes a series of recordings with Columbia Records.

Artur Schnabel publishes *My Life in Music*.

1963
In Washington, D.C. 200,000 black and white "freedom marchers" demonstrate.

Lester B. Pearson is elected prime minister of Canada.

In November, U.S. President John F. Kennedy is assassinated in

A Musical Force

Gould and His Times

In July, he gives the inaugural MacMillan Lectures at the University of Toronto.

In August he performs twice at the Stratford Festival.

1964
On April 10, Gould performs at the Wilshire Ebell Theatre in Los Angeles. This will be his last live public performance.

On June 1, the University of Toronto awards him an Honorary Doctor of Laws degree, and he delivers the convocation address, "An Argument for Music in the Electronic Age."

His recordings released this year include Bach, Two- and Three-Part Inventions and *The Well-Tempered Clavier*, Book I, Nos. 9–16.

On November 11, he addresses the graduating class of the Royal Conservatory of Music.

1965
CBC Radio broadcasts *Dialogues on the Prospects of Recording*, a documentary written and narrated by Glenn Gould.

Canada and the World

Dallas, Texas. He is succeeded by Lyndon Baines Johnson.

1964
American civil rights leader Martin Luther King wins the Nobel Peace Prize.

Leonid Brezhnev replaces Nikita Khrushchev as Chairman of the Council of Ministers in the U.S.S.R. The Cold War intensifies.

Marshall McLuhan's *Understanding Media: The Extensions of Man* is published.

A future international star, Canadian jazz pianist and singer Diana Krall, is born in Nanaimo, B.C.

Beatlemania sweeps North America after the Beatles appear on the *Ed Sullivan Show*.

1965
In the U.S., racial violence occurs in Selma, Alabama and the Watts district of Los Angeles.

Glenn Gould

Gould and His Times

Gould's recordings released this year include Bach's *The Well-Tempered Clavier*, Book I, Nos. 17–24.

1966
On November 13, Gould's weekly CBC Radio show, *The Art of Glenn Gould*, begins.

His recordings released this year include Beethoven's Piano Concerto no. 5 in E-flat Major, *Emperor*, with Leopold Stokowski conducting the American Symphony Orchestra, and Schoenberg's *The Book of the Hanging Gardens*, with soprano Helen Vanni.

1967
Walter Homburger's role as Gould's manager ends.

Columbia releases Gould's recording of Schoenberg's *Ode to Napoleon Bonaparte*, op. 41, with

Canada and the World

American students demonstrate against the escalating war in Vietnam.

Vladimir Horowitz returns with a legendary twenty-fifth anniversary concert at Carnegie Hall. Millions view this performance in a TV special, *Vladimir Horowitz at Carnegie Hall*.

Canada adopts the Maple Leaf flag.

1966
Indira Gandhi becomes prime minister of India.

In Canada, the Medical Care Act is passed.

Colour TV is introduced in Canada.

1967
The Six Day War, a new Arab-Israeli conflict, erupts in the Middle East.

Canada hosts the World's Fair Expo 67 in Montreal to celebrate Canada's centenary.

A Musical Force

Gould and His Times

the Juilliard String Quintet and John Horton, narrator.

The CBC broadcasts *The Idea of North*, the first part of the Glenn Gould trilogy dealing with solitude. This is Gould's first broadcast involving contrapuntal radio.

1968
Gould hosts a weekly TV series called *World of Music* from February 4 to March 17.

Columbia releases an album titled *Glenn Gould: Concert Dropout,* Glenn Gould in Conversation with John McClure.

Robert Fulford becomes editor of *Saturday Night* magazine, a position he will hold until 1987.

Canada and the World

President Charles De Gaulle of France visits Montreal and shouts "*Vive le Québec libre!*"

Canadian poet Leonard Cohen moves to the U.S. and begins a career as a singer-songwriter with the release of his first album, *Songs of Leonard Cohen.*

1968
Warsaw Pact troops invade Prague, ending Czech hopes of liberation from the Soviet yoke.

Pierre Elliott Trudeau succeeds Lester Pearson as prime minister of Canada. The general election that follows is dominated by "Trudeau-mania," and the Liberals form a majority government.

René Lévesque founds the Parti Québécois.

In the U.S., civil rights leader Martin Luther King and presidential candidate Robert Kennedy are assassinated. Republican Richard Nixon is elected president.

147

Glenn Gould

Gould and His Times

1969
On September 9, the Canada Council awards Glenn Gould the Molson Prize.

On November 12, CBC Radio *Ideas* broadcasts *The Latecomers*, a radio documentary on Newfoundland. This is the second part of Gould's trilogy on solitude.

1970
CBC-TV airs two Gould films: on February 18, *The Well-Tempered Listener* and on August 5, the film version of *The Idea of North*.

1971
Gould begins to use the Eaton Auditorium in Toronto as a recording studio.

On February 2, the CBC airs Gould's radio documentary *Stokowski: A Portrait for Radio*.

The CD 318 concert grand piano on loan to Gould from Steinway is damaged while being moved and is repaired at the factory.

1972
Gould arranges the music for the film *Slaughterhouse-Five*, based on the novel by Kurt Vonnegut.

Canada and the World

1969
American astronaut Neil Armstrong is the first human being to walk on the moon.

Following the recommendations of the Royal Commission on Bilingualism and Biculturalism, Canada's Parliament passes the Official Languages Act. French and English are declared the official languages of Canada.

1970
In Canada, Prime Minister Trudeau invokes the War Measures Act during the October Crisis in Quebec.

1971
Greenpeace is founded in Vancouver, Canada.

1972
The Watergate break-in scandal erupts during the U.S. presidential campaign.

A Musical Force

Gould and His Times

He meets Bruno Monsaingeon, who proposes to film him for French television as a "great personality of music." They make four films together as part of a series, *Chemins de la Musique*.

1973
Gould finally buys his Steinway concert grand piano, CD 318.

Gould releases six new albums. He wins a GRAMMY Award for best album notes, classical, for *Hindemith, The Piano Sonatas Complete*.

1974
Monsaingeon's films of Gould are broadcast in France, and his record sales there increase significantly.

CBC-TV *Musicamera* begins the series *Music in Our Time*, in which Gould will discuss modern music, decade by decade. No. 1, "The Age of Ecstasy, 1900–1910" is broadcast in February.

Gould prepares a series of ten radio programs entitled *Music of Today: Schoenberg Series*, which is broadcast on the CBC between September 11 and November 13.

Canada and the World

In the Canadian federal election Pierre Elliott Trudeau and the Liberals are re-elected as a minority government.

1973
The Americans withdraw from Vietnam, and Saigon falls to the Communist forces.

The Israeli-Arab conflict in the Middle East (Yom Kippur War), leads to an increase in the price of oil.

1974
U.S president Richard Nixon is forced to resign as a result of his role in the Watergate cover up.

In the Canadian federal election, Trudeau's Liberals win a majority government.

Glenn Gould

Gould and His Times

1975
Glenn Gould's parents sell the cottage at Lake Simcoe.

Florence Gould suffers a massive stroke and dies.

Around this time, Ray Roberts becomes Gould's friend and part-time assistant.

CBC-TV *Musicamera* broadcasts two programs in Gould's *Music in our Time* series: No. 2, "The Flight from Order: Music from 1910 to 1920" and No. 3, "New Faces, Old Forms: Music from 1920 to 1930."

1976
The Canadian Conference of the Arts awards Glenn Gould the *Diplôme d'honneur*.

Gould is diagnosed with hypertension.

He worries about recurring pain and stiffness in his hands causing problems with his playing.

1977
The *Quiet in the Land* airs on CBC Radio *Ideas* on March 25. This is the third part of Gould's trilogy dealing with solitude.

Canada and the World

1975
The Helsinki Accord is signed by thirty-five leaders from Europe and North America. It reduces political and military tension between East and West in the Cold War and contains important provisions related to human rights.

1976
Democrat Jimmy Carter is elected president of the U.S.

Vietnam is reunified.

In Canada, a separatist Parti Québécois government led by René Lévesque is elected in Quebec.

Montreal hosts the Olympic Games.

1977
In the U.S., NASA launches the twin spacecraft *Voyager 1* and *Voyager 2* from Cape Canaveral, Florida.

A Musical Force

Gould and His Times

CBC-TV *Musicamera* broadcasts No. 4 in the *Music in Our Time* series, "The Artist as Artisan, 1930–1940."

1978
Glenn Gould: Music and Mind by Geoffrey Payzant is published in Toronto. Gould reviews the book in the *Globe and Mail*.

1979
Gould declines his father's invitation to act as best man at his wedding to Vera Dobson, a family friend.

1980
Bert Gould remarries. Glenn does not attend the wedding.

The *Glenn Gould Silver Jubilee Album*, a two-record set, is released by CBS Records (Columbia Records).

Canada and the World

Elvis Presley dies from an overdose of prescription drugs at his Memphis home, Graceland.

1979
In Canada, Joe Clark's Progressive Conservative Party wins a minority government but remains in power for less than one year.

Margaret Thatcher becomes the first woman prime minister of Great Britain.

Voyager 1 and *Voyager 2* approach Jupiter and make a number of important discoveries.

1980
Republican Ronald Reagan, a former actor, is elected president of the U.S.

In Canada, the Liberals under Trudeau return to power.

The first Quebec referendum on sovereignty association with the rest of Canada results in a "no" victory.

151

Glenn Gould

Gould and His Times

1981
Gould receives the Canadian Music Council Medal.

He buys a Yamaha CF concert grand piano.

1982
Gould's second recording of the *Goldberg Variations* is released.

He arranges the music for the feature film *The Wars*, based on the novel by Timothy Findley.

In August, Gould records the chamber version of Richard Wagner's *Siegfried Idyll* for CBS. This recording marks the beginning of his new career as a conductor.

On September 25, Gould turns fifty. On September 27, he suffers a massive stroke.

On October 4, in Toronto, Glenn Gould dies. He is buried in Mount Pleasant Cemetery.

1983
The *Goldberg Variations* wins two GRAMMY Awards and a JUNO Award.

Canada and the World

1981
The Canadian Conference of the Arts awards Robert Fulford the *Diplôme d'honneur*.

Voyager 1 and *Voyager 2* fly by Saturn and study its rings and the atmospheres of both the planet and its moon Titan.

1982
The Constitution Act, 1982 to patriate and amend Canada's Constitution, is signed by the Queen.

In the U.S.S.R., Leonid Brezhnev dies, and Yuri Andropov is appointed general secretary of the Communist Party.

The Falklands War takes place between Britain and Argentina.

1983
In the U.S., the first test flight of the space shuttle *Columbia* takes place.

A Musical Force

Gould and His Times

Glenn Gould is posthumously inducted into the Canadian Music Hall of Fame.

The Glenn Gould Foundation is created to establish and support projects to provide a memorial to Gould and his work.

1984
The *Goldberg Variations* wins a Gold Disc award given by the Canadian Recording Industry Association.

1986
The Glenn Gould Foundation establishes the Glenn Gould Prize in Music and Communication.

Canada and the World

Drought in Ethiopia causes famine and suffering that affects millions of people.

1984
John Turner succeeds Pierre Elliott Trudeau as leader of the Liberal Party and as prime minister of Canada. In the election that follows in September, Brian Mulroney's Conservatives defeat the Liberals.

Indian prime minister Indira Gandhi is assassinated by her Sikh bodyguards.

1986
In the U.S., the space shuttle *Challenger* explodes right after it is launched, killing all seven crew members.

The prime minister of Sweden, Olof Palme, is assassinated by a lone gunman.

Voyager 2 flies by Uranus and discovers ten previously unknown moons.

Glenn Gould

Gould and His Times   *Canada and the World*

2007–2008
The International Year of Glenn Gould begins on September 25, the twenty-fifth anniversary of his death. The year of celebrations commemorated the fiftieth anniversary of Gould's performances in the Soviet Union and the seventy-fifth anniversary of his birth.

Acknowledgements

Several people helped me write this book. Rhonda Bailey, editorial director, encouraged me from the start and offered wise writing advice through the various drafts. Frank McCormick read the initial draft and offered many words of encouragement. John Wilson and Tom Shardlow, fellow contributors to this series, commented frequently on early drafts and helped me keep my eye on the final goal. Roberta Starke read the entire manuscript several times and provided detailed comments after each reading. Kevin Bazzana kindly answered several technical questions. My wife, Leslie Davidge, never once wavered in her support.

In depicting Glenn Gould's life and work, I have relied chiefly on the following sources for biographical detail and dialogue: Kevin Bazzana's superb biography *Wondrous Strange: The Life and Art of Glenn Gould*; Otto Friedrich's *Glenn Gould: A Life and Variations*; John McGreevy's *Glenn Gould: Variations*; Peter F. Ostwald's *Glenn Gould: The Ecstasy and Tragedy of Genius*; and the National Film Board of Canada's documentaries *Glenn Gould: Off the Record* and *Glenn Gould: On the Record*. Any errors are my own.

Sources Consulted

Books

Bazzana, Kevin. *The Performer in the Work*. Oxford: Clarendon Press, 1997.

Bazzana, Kevin. *Wondrous Strange: The Life and Art of Glenn Gould*. Toronto: McClelland & Stewart Ltd., 2003.

Carroll, Jock. *Glenn Gould: Some Portraits of the Artist as a Young Man*. Toronto: Stoddard, 1995.

Cott, Jonathan. *Conversations with Glenn Gould*. Little, Brown & Company (Canada) Limited, 1984.

Friedrich, Otto. *Glenn Gould: A Life and Variations*. Toronto: Lester & Orpen Dennys, 1989.

Grout, Donald Jay. *A History of Western Music*. Revised Edition. New York: W.W. Norton & Company, 1973.

Kazdin, Andrew: *Glenn Gould: Creative Lying*. New York: E.P Dutton, 1989.

Konieczny, Vladimir. *Struggling for Perfection: The Story of Glenn Gould*. Toronto: Napoleon Publishing, 2004.

McGreevy, John. *Glenn Gould: Variations*. Doubleday Canada, 1983.

Ostwald, Peter. F. *Glenn Gould: The Tragedy and the Ecstasy of Genius*. New York: W.W. Norton & Company, 1997.

Page, Tim. ed. *The Glenn Gould Reader*. Toronto: Lester & Orpen Dennys, 1984.

Payzant, Geoffrey. *Glenn Gould: Music & Mind*. Toronto: Van Nostrand Reinhold Ltd., 1978.

Powe, B.W. *The Solitary Outlaw. Trudeau, Lewis, Gould, Canetti, McLuhan*. Toronto: Lester & Orpen Dennys, 1987.

Rosen, Charles. *The Classical Style: Haydn, Mozart, Beethoven*. New York/London: W. W. Norton & Company, 1971.

Roy, Lynette. *The Genius and His Music*. Toronto: Canadian Heroes Series: University of Toronto Press, 1999.

Pamphlets, Articles, and Book Chapters

Addison, Angela, "The Ultimate Soloist: A Portrait of Glenn Gould," Bulletin of the Glenn Gould Society: Groningen, The Netherlands, (October 1988).

Centre Culturel Canadien. *Glenn Gould*. Paris: Sur Les Presses De L'Imprimerie Georges Michel, 1986.

Mesaros, Helen. "Glenn Gould Makes Music: Glory and Plight of a Concert Pianist." National Archives of Canada.

Phillips, Rick, "Man, Musician, Myth, and Mystique." Gramophone, Vol. 80, no. 56 (August 2002), p. 27–29.

Films

Glenn Gould: Off the Record. National Film Board of Canada. 1960.

Glenn Gould: On the Record. National Film Board of Canada. 1960.

Index

Page numbers in *italics* indicate photographs

ACTRA Awards, *114*
"The Age of Ecstasy, 1900–1910," 149
American Symphony Orchestra, 146
The Anatomy of the Fugue, 144
anti-Semitism in Canada, 10
"An Argument for Music in the Electronic Age," 145
Arnold Schoenberg: A Perspective, 144
Arnold Schoenberg: The Man Who Changed Music, 107, 144
Arrau, Claudio, 24, 29
Art Gallery of Ontario, 47, 51
Art Gallery of Toronto, 51
"The Artist as Artisan, 1930–1940", 151
The Art of Glenn Gould, 146
Austria, 87, 130, 131, 141

Bach, Johann Sebastian, 7, 34, 44–46, *50*, 66, 70, 85, 92, 98, 104, 108, 117, 127
   The Art of the Fugue, 3
   Concerto in D Minor, 93
   Goldberg Variations, viii, 64, 72–76, 80, 81, 86, 100, 119, 125, 126, 139, 152, 153
   Italian Concerto, 93
   Partita in D Major, 3
   Partita no. 5 in G Major, 70, 80
   Partita no. 6, 85
   Prelude and Fugue in C Major, 127
   The Well-Tempered Clavier, 24, 72, 127, 145, 146
Badura-Skoda, Paul, 69
Bahamas, 76
Banquo (dog), 86, 87
BBC, 100, 130, 142
Beach, the, 9, 10, 54
Beckwith, John, 40
Beethoven, Ludwig von, 3, 34, 36, 71, 80, 81, 85, 86, 91, 108, 121, 130
   "Ghost" Trio, 65
   Piano Concerto no. 2, 81, 91, 121
   Piano Concerto no. 3, 80, 82, 87, 89
   Piano Concerto no. 4, 29, 31, 33, 79, 80, 135
   Piano Concerto no. 5, "Emperor", 80, 146
   Sonata no. 30 in E Major, 3, 66, 70
Berg, Alban, 43, 44, 47, 70
   Sonata, Opus 1, 85, 86
Berlin, 84, 87, 143, 141
Berlin Philharmonic Orchestra, 87, 93, 141

Glenn Gould

Bernstein, Felicia, 82
Bernstein, Leonard, 75, 81, 82, 99, 140, 144
Bolshoi Hall, 141
Boston, 89, 91
Brahms, Johannes, 86, 100, 121
  Piano Concerto no. 1 in D Minor, 99, 144
Brando, Marlon, 104
Buffalo, 89
Burton, Humphrey, 100
Business Men's Bible Class, 13
Busoni, Ferruccio Benvenuto, 87

CBS Records, *viii*, 97, 151, 152
Caledon Hills, 100
Calgary, 51
Calgary Women's Musical Club, 137
Canada, 32, 63, 67, 75, 83, 92, 129 133, 135–141, 144, 146–153
Canada Council, 63, 126, 140, 148
Canadian Broadcasting Corporation (CBC), 131
  CBC Opera Company, 63
  CBC Radio, 19, 47, 61, 66, 72, *102*, 104, 105–107, 132, 137, 144–150
  CBC Symphony Orchestra, 63
  CBC Television, 104, 117, *124*, 126, 138, 143, 147–151
Canadian Centennial, 105
Canadian Conference of the Arts, 126, 150, 152
Canadian Embassy, Moscow, 84
Canadian League of Composers, 63
Canadian Music Centre, 63
Canadian Music Council, 63, 126
Canadian Music Council Medal, 126, 152
Canadian Music Hall of Fame, 126, 153
Canadian National Exhibition, 20
Canadian North, 104, 105
Canadian Press, 84
Canadian Recording Industry Association, 126, 153

Carnegie Hall, 140, 144, 146
Carroll, Jock, 67, 76
Casavant organ, 25
Chemins de la Musique, 149
Chickering piano, *50*, 62, 91, 95
Chopin, Frédéric, 7, 14, 34, 43, 44, 49, 71
Cincinnati, 144
Cities: Glenn Gould's Toronto, 114
Cleveland Orchestra, 82, 83, 140
Cliburn, Van, 56, 141, 142
Cold War, 84, 135, 143, 150
Columbia Records, 69, 73, 80, 92, 93, 108, 119, 139, 144, 146, 147, 151
Copeland, Aaron, 75
Corbett Music Lecture, 144
Cott, Johnathan, 105, 118
cottage, *16*, 41, *50*, 53, 57, 59, 62, 64, 65, 67, 96, 109, 133, 150
Couperin, Francis, 34
Credit River, 100

The Daily Woof, 19
Dallas, 80
Detroit Free Press, 79
Detroit Symphony Orchestra, 79, 139
Dialogue on the Prospects of Recording, 145
Dieppe, 19, 133
Dobson, Vera, 118, 122, 151
Donchery, 94, 142
Dudley, Ray, 20, 35, 36, 51, 95

East General Hospital, 113
Eaton Centre, 118
Eaton Auditorium, 25, 34, 51, 108, 109, 134, 135, 148
Emmanuel Presbyterian Church, 13
Empire Club, 34
Europe, 88, 91–94, 96, 134, 142
Evans, Bill, 108
Evening Telegram, 33

Fantasia (Disney film), 87
Feore, Colin, 125

162

A Musical Force

Findley, Timothy, 119, 120, 152
finger-tapping technique, 40, 64, 73
Fitzgerald, Winston, 95
"The Flight from Order: Music from 1910 to 1920," 150
Forrester, Maureen, 52
Fort Churchill, 104
Foss, Cornelia, 111, 112
Foss, Lukas, 111
Frankfort, 87
Fulford, Robert, 19, 25, 44, 51, 54, 62–64, 110, 132, 137, 138, 144, 147, 152
Fulford, Wayne, 36

Germany, 32, 87, 129–132, 134, 138, 141
Gibbons, Orlando, 44, 70
Glamour magazine, 75
Glenn Gould: A Portrait, 126
Glenn Gould: Concert Dropout, 147
The Glenn Gould Foundation, 153
Glenn Gould: Music and Mind, 151
Glenn Gould: Off the Record, 93, 143
Glenn Gould: On the Record, 93, 143
The Glenn Gould Prize for Music and Communication, 153
The Glenn Gould Reader, 117
The Glenn Gould Silver Jubilee Album, 151
Globe and Mail, 34, 76, 137, 151
Gold, Thomas (paternal great-grandfather), 10
Gold Standard Furs, 9, 14, 17
Goldberg Variations. *See* Bach, Johann Sebastian
Gordon Thompson Scholarship, 25, 134
Gould, Glenn Herbert
    adolescence, 28–57, 135–137
    album, program notes, 80, 97, 149
    alter egos, 104
    ambition to be concert pianist, 13, 14, 52, 55, 56, 75
    antisocial tendency, 17, 18, 71
    appearance, 2, 3, 29, 34, 55, 119, 120
    awards, honours, 24, 126, 133, 134,
    142, 145, 148–150, 152
    birth, 5, 7, 9, 129
    cancels concerts, 1, 92, 95, 96
    celebrity, 75–77
    childhood, 3, 6, 7–15, *16*, 17–26, 129, 131–134
    communicator, 97, 98, 104, 126, 140
    composes, 13, 42, 46, 65, 66, 136, 139
    concerts, recitals, 31–36, 46, 47, 51, 63, 64, 67, 70, 71, 75, 77, 79–82, 84–87, 89, 91–94, 96, 98–100
    conducts, 121, 122, 152
    "contrapuntal radio," 105, 106, 147
    debut with Toronto Symphony, 33, 135
    discovers contemporary music, 41–47, 136
    dislike of audiences, pressure, 52, 96
    dislike of competitions, competitiveness, 52, 59, 96, 97, 117
    dissatisfaction with concerts, live music, 96, 97
    dissatisfaction with pianos, 31, 41, 80, 91, 95, 108
    eccentric dresser, 4, 20, 61, 65, 73, 82, 83, 91, 98
    education, 14, 15, 17–19, 32, 35–37, 53, 54, 131, 132
    film soundtracks, 116, 119, 120, 148, 152
    films on, 93, 108, 119, 125, 126, 143, 149
    final concert, 4, 101, 145
    first booking as soloist, 34, 35, 135
    first concert attended, 13, 14, 131
    first performances, 13, 24, 25, 26, 36, 37, 131, 135–137
    first recording, 71–76, 79
    genius, 44, 62
    germ phobia, 19, 20, 112, 113
    hand-soaking before performances, 1, 2, 70

163

hypochondria, 70, 95, 96, 108, 112, 115, 116
illness, 76, 91, 92, 96, 112, 115, 116, 120, 150
independent, stubborn streak, 64–66, 103
loner, private person, 57–59, 63, 111
love affair, 111, 112
love of animals, 17, 19, 22, 111, 119, 120
love of children, 110, 111
love of recording, studio, 47, 48, 97, 99, *102*
love of words, lecturing, writing, 19, 35, 36, 53, 54, 83, 86, 97, 98, 104, 117, 144, 145
math whiz, 35, 43, 104
medications, 2, 70, 79, 83, 99, 112, 115
middle-class background, 9, 10
moves to cottage, 59–67, 138
musical prodigy, 7, 8, 10–13, 23
perfect pitch, 11
phenomenal memory, 53, 62, 64, 65
piano chair, 1, 3, 4, 65, 73, 81–83
piano lessons from mother, 7, 10–12, 129
piano style, technique, 4, 18, 30, 31, 35, 39, 40, 56, 57, 64, 67, 73, 126
plays organ, 18, 24, 53, 133, 134
plays on radio, television, 25, 47, 134, 137, 138
posthumous honours, 126, 152–154
practising in his head, 31
pressures of performing, touring, 76, 77, 89, 91
produces concerts, 63, 138, 139
puritanical tendencies, 45, 54
quits school, 54, 55, 138
radio and television programs for CBC, 104, 105, 106, 107, *114*, 116, 117, 144–151
recording activities, 71–76, 79, 80, 93, 97, 98, 104, 107–109, 116, 119, 122, 139, 145–149, 152
reviews, 26, 32, 33, 35, 66, 70, 71, 79, 81, 87, 94, 99, 144
Sonata for Bassoon and Piano, 46, 137
Sonata for Piano, 46, 136
spinal injury, 20, 53, 96, 133
stage anxiety, 2, 3, 34, 52, 53, 99
stage mannerisms, 1, 3, 4, 33, 51, 52, 56, 79, 82, 83, 89, 92, 98
String Quartet in F Minor, Opus 1, 66, 116, 139
stroke and death, 122, 123, 152
studies, wins medals at Toronto Conservatory, 18, 24
sues Steinway & Sons, 96
Toronto Conservatory Associate Diploma, 25, 134, 135
U.S. debut, *68*, 69–71, 75, 139
views on music, composers, 29, 30, 42–46, 49, 51, 80, 126
wild driver, 61, 75, 76, 91, 110, 111
Gould, Florence Emma (mother), 5, *8*, 10–14, 16, 17, 20, 21, 23, 24, 27, 31, 42, 45, 54–57, 59, 63, 69 129, 135, 150; controlling, 20, 51, 53, 59; musical ambitions for Glenn, 6–8; piano teacher to Glenn, 7–10, 23, 72, 129; religious, 10; stroke and death, 113, 114, 118, 150
Gould, Russell Herbert, "Bert" (father), 5, 9, 11–13, 17, 21, 23, 29, 31, 36, 40, 41, 54–57, 61, 63, 69, 71, 113, 122, 123, 129, 135, 150; played violin, 7; religious, 10; second marriage, 118, 151
Graffman, Gary, 56, 69, 71, 135
GRAMMY Awards, 126, 149, 152
Great Depression, 5, 9, 129
Grieg, Edvard, 8, 108
Greig, Jessie (cousin), 27, 29, 55, 56, 114, 120, 122, 123, 134

Grieg, Mary (maternal great-grandmother), 8, 52
Guerrero, Alberto, 24, 30, 32, 34, 39, 40–43, 52, 53, 55–57, 72, 133, 136, 138; death, 94, 95, 142
Guerrero, Myrtle Rose, 39, 57

Hamburg, 91
Hamilton Philharmonic Orchestra, 121
The Hamptons, 111
Harriet Cohen Bach Medal, *90*, 92, 126, 142
Hart House, 51
Haydn, Joseph, 7, 34, 44, 108
Heinze, Bernard, *28*, 135
High Fidelity magazine, 104, 117
Hindemith, Paul, 3, 42–44, 46, 47, 108, 129, 132
  Matthias the Painter (opera), 42, 129
  Sonata no. 3, 3, 47, 86
Hofmann, Josef, 13, 14, 33, 131
Homberger, Walter, 2, 3, 32, 34, 63, 69, 71, 75, 84, 135, 146
Horowitz, Vladimir, 14, 29, 49, 56, 132, 138, 144, 146
Hudson Bay, 104
Hume, Paul, 70
Hupfer, William, 95, 96
Hurricane Hazel, 64, 139

"The Idea of North", 107, *124*, 148
Ideas, 148, 150
Inn on the Park, 94
International Artists Series, 34, 135
International Year of Glenn Gould, 154
Israel, 89, 91, 92, 141
Italy, 141

Jerusalem, 91
JUNO Awards, 126, 152

Kappell, William, 69
Karajan, Herbert von, 75, 87, 88, 93, 94, 141

Kasments, Udo, 98
Kazdin, Andrew, 107, 110
Keckes, Marilyn, 111
Kensington Market, 118
Keyboard Town, 12
Keyserling, Count Hermann Karl von, 72
Kilbonoff, John, 121
Kilburn, Nicholas, 46
Kiwanis Music Festival, 24, 25, 52, 133, 134
Krenel, Ernst, 86

Lake Ontario, 9
Lake Simcoe, 14, *16*, 20–23, *50*, 133, 138, 150
Landowski, Wanda, 64, 66, 72, 74
"The Latecomers," 107, 148
Leacock, Stephen, 20
Leipzig, 72
Leningrad, 84, 86, 88, 141
Leningrad Philharmonic Orchestra, 141
"Let's Ban Applause," 144
Leventritt, Rosalie, 71
Life magazine, 75
Liszt, Franz, 14, 34, 43
Little, Carl, 62
Little, Clarence, 20
London, England, 92, 93, 100
London, Ontario, 137
London Symphony Orchestra, 142
Los Angeles, 1, 4, 101, 138, 145
Lower Rosedale Shakespeare Reading and Badminton Society, 88
Lucerne, 93, 142
Lucerne Philharmonia, 93, 142

MacLean, Wally, 104, 105
MacMillan Lectures, 145
Mahler, Gustav, 117
Maloney, Timothy, 122
Malvern Collegiate Institute, 35, 36, 53, 54, 134, 136, 138
Massey, Vincent, 52

Glenn Gould

Massey Hall, 13, *28*, 76, 131, 135
Masterworks series, 108
McGreevy, John, 117
McGregors (maternal ancestors), 10
Melinda Street, 14
Mendelssohn, Felix, 34, 43
Menuhin, Yehudi, 12, 116
Molson Prize, 126, 148
Monsaingeon, Bruno, 108, 119, 149
Montreal, 51, 66, 75, 139, 143, 146, 147, 150
Montreal Symphony Orchestra, 139
Moose Jaw, 47
Morawetz, Oskar, 44, 64
    Fantasy in D, 64, 65
Moscow, 84, 85, 141, 142
Moscow Philharmonic Orchestra, 85
Moscow State Conservatory, 85, 140
Mount Pleasant Cemetery, 125–127, 152
Mozart, Wolfgang Amadeus, 7, 11, 13, 41, 42, 43, 49, 71, 91, 108
    Symphony no. 40 in G Minor, 42
The Music of Man, 116
Music of Today: Schoenberg Series, 149
Music in our Time, 149–151
"Music in the West," 141
Musicamera, 149–151
Muskeg Express, 104

National Academy of Recording Arts and Sciences, 126
National Ballet of Canada, 63
National Film Board of Canada (NFB), 93, 131, 132, 143
Nazis, 19, 130, 134
Neo-classical music, 98
Nelsova, Zara, 65
New Brunswick, 138
"New Faces, Old Forms: Music from 1920 to 1930", 150
New Music Associates, 63, 138, 139
New York City, *viii*, 68, 69, 71, 72, 75, 92, 95, 108, 119, 121, 136, 139

New York Herald Tribune, 100
New York Philharmonic Orchestra, 81, 99, 140, 144
New York Times, 81, 83, 144
Newfoundland, 107, 132, 136, 148
Newmarket, 34
Nicky (dog), 19, 21, 22, 33, 47
North. *See* Canadian North
North America, 92, 97, 141, 150
Northern Ontario, 107

Olnick, Harry, 66, 71, 72
On to Ottawa trek, 9, 129
Ontario, 13, 20, 34, 61, 79
Ontario Science Centre, 118
Oppenheim, David, 69, 71
Orillia, 20, 61
Ostwald, Peter F., 66, 67, 110
Ottawa, 51, 75

Pasadena, 80
Payzant, Geoffrey, 151
A Piano Lesson with Glenn Gould, 98
The Piano Quarterly, 109, 117
Phillips Gallery, 70, 139
Plummer, Christopher, 98
Poulenc, Francis, 45
Prokofiev, Sergei, 45, 47, 108
    Sonata no. 7 in B-flat Major

Quebec, 84, 133, 139, 142, 148, 150, 151
"The Quiet in the Land," 107, 150

Rachmaninov, Sergei, 14, 35, 49
Regina, 9, 129
Richard Strauss: The Bourgeois Hero, 107
Roberts, John, 94, 100, 110, 111
Roberts, Ray, 109–111, 115, 120, 122, 150
Robyn, Louise, 12
Romanticism, 14, 43, 44, 46
Royal Conservatory of Music (Toronto), 18, 25, 46, 108, 145
Royal Conservatory Opera School, 63

166

Royal York Hotel, 34
Rubenstein, Arthur, 14, 29, 56, 103, 135
Russia, 78, 84–87, 132

Salzburg, 91, 93
San Francisco, 80
Scarlatti, Domenico, 34
Schnabel, Arthur, 29, 30, 32, 130, 134, 144
Schneider, Alexander, 65, 69
Schoenberg, Arnold, 41–45, 47, 63, 85, 86, 98, 107, 108, 130, 133, 136; death, 138
  The Book of the Hanging Gardens, 146
  Ode to Napoleon Bonaparte, 146
  Symphony no. 40 in G Minor, 42
Schonberg, Harold, 81, 83, 144
Schubert, Franz, 49
Scott, Howard, 80
Second World War, 9, 19, 63, 84, 131–134
serial music, 43, 44
Serkin, Rudolf, 66
Seto, Bill, 61, 100
Shangri-La Gardens, 61, 100
Siegfried Idyll, 122, 152
Silverman, Robert, 109
Silvester, Frederick, 18, 24, 133
Simpson's Department Store, 34
Slaughterhouse-Five, 116, 148
Smith, Leo, 24, 132, 133
32 Southwood Drive, 9
Soviet Union (U.S.S.R.), 78, 84, 85, 138–141, 144, 145, 152, 154. *See also* Russia
St. Clair Avenue West, 94, 109, 110, 142
Steinway CD 318 piano, 95, 108, 143, 148, 149
Steinway, Frederick, 96
Steinway & Sons, 95, 96, 108
St. Louis, 80
Stokowski: A Portrait for Radio, 107, 148
Stokowski, Leopold, 87, 88, 107, 146
St. Petersburg, 84. *See also* Leningrad

Stratford, Ontario, 79, 80
Stratford Festival, 65, 69, 72, 98, 138, 143, 145
Strauss, Richard, 107
St. Simon's Anglican Church, 53
Sunshine Sketches of a Little Town, 20
Sweden, 141
Sweelinck, Jan Pieterszoon, 70
  "Fitzwilliam" Fantasia, 70
Szell, George, 82, 83

Tchaikovsky Hall, 86, 140
Tel Aviv, 89
Thirty-two Short Films about Glenn Gould, 125
Toronto, 8–10, 13, 14, 22–25, 28, 34, 43, 46, 53, 63, 64, 66, 75, 79, 88, 94, 110, 111, *114*, 117–119, 129, 131, 134, 135, 137–139, 142, 148
Toronto Conservatory of Music (TCM), 18, 24, 25, 33, 132, 133. *See also* Royal Conservatory of Music
Toronto Conservatory Orchestra, 29, 31, 32
Toronto Daily Star, 33, 71, 98. *See also Toronto Star*
Toronto General Hospital, 113, 122
Toronto Star, 61, 110. *See also Toronto Daily Star*
Toronto Symphony Orchestra, 33, 51, *102*
Toronto Symphony Orchestra Secondary School Concert, 28
Toronto Telegram, 100
Toronto Zoo, 117
Town Hall recital, 68, 69, 139
Tulk, Lorne, 106, 110, 113
Tureck, Roslyn, 64, 72, 74
Twelfth Night, 37, 136
twelve-tone system, 43, 44, 130

United Church, 10
United States, 67, 75, 80, 83, 111, 129–133, 138–145, 148–153

University of Cincinnati, 144
University of Toronto, 72, 137, 145
University of Western Ontario, 137
Uptergrove, 20, 62, 91–93
U.S.S.R. *See* Soviet Union
Uxbridge, 8, 13
Uxbridge United Church, 131

Vancouver, 51, 83, 148
Vancouver International Festival, 143
Vancouver Symphony Orchestra, 137
Vanni, Helen, 146
Vienna, 84, 87, 88, 141
Vienna Festival, 141
Vogue magazine, 75
Vonnegut, Kurt, 116, 148
Voyager 1 and *2*, spacecraft, 127, 150, 151, 152, 153

Wagner, Richard, 42, 122, 152
The Wars, 119, 120, 152
Washington, D.C., 70, 139, 144
The Well-Tempered Listener, 148
Williamson Road Elementary Public School, 14, 131, 132
Wilshire Ebell Theatre, 1, 101, 145
Windsor Arms Hotel, 94, 142
Winnipeg, 51
Winnipeg Symphony Orchestra, 77
The World of Music, 147

Yamaha piano, 108, 152
Yazbeck, Paul, 51